Hampton Roads

CHRONICLES

Hampton Roads

CHRONICLES

HISTORY FROM THE
BIRTHPLACE OF AMERICA

PAUL CLANCY

THE
History
PRESS

Published by The History Press
Charleston, SC 29403
www.historypress.net

Cover design by Natasha Momberger

First published 2009

ISBN 978.1.54023.433.9

Library of Congress Cataloging-in-Publication Data

Clancy, Paul R., 1939-
Hampton Roads chronicles : history from the birthplace of America / Paul Clancy.
p. cm.
ISBN 978.1.54023.433.9
1. Hampton Roads (Va. : Region)--History. 2. Hampton Roads (Va. : Region)--Social life
and customs. I. Title.
F232.H23C547 2009
975.5'5--dc22
2009007730

For Barbara

CONTENTS

Contents

PREFACE

T ake a stroll with me. Stand on the high dunes at Cape Henry and
imagine, out there where the stupendous energy of the ocean moves
with the rhythm of the tides, the beginning of America. The arrival of
English settlers, the collision of cultures, the struggle for survival, the
birth of independence, the clash of arms—it all starts here. And, like the
tide, history flows through every corner of Hampton Roads. Take your
history dipper with you beside the James, the Elizabeth, the Nansemond,
the York, the Dismal Swamp Canal and you can ladle it up by the gallon,
by the hogshead.

There are fabulous museums and historic homes in Norfolk, Portsmouth,
Chesapeake, Virginia Beach and Suffolk, in Hampton, Newport News,
Jamestown and Williamsburg. The local history collections in public libraries
are brimming with stories and anecdotes.

Take in exhibits on early Indian settlements and feel the tug of a pre–Ice
Age past; check out the digs at Jamestown, where the bones and pottery
shards of an almost tragic beginning remain, and be dragged into their
forensic labyrinth; walk the battlefields at Yorktown and the Peninsula;
sail the waters anywhere in the region where warships clashed and rode at
anchor. The elements of history come rushing at you with open arms.

The stories of the region are often drenched in gore and intrigue. Who
would have thought that a simple name like Bennett's Creek would take you
back to the beheading of a king of England? Who could imagine that the
founder of a plantation in old Princess Anne County might have been mixed
up with rum and slaves in Barbados? That graffiti and bloodstains in the
upper rooms of a mansion in Suffolk would betoken a tragic war? That an
alley in downtown Norfolk might have provided the setting for a sensational
murder trial?

But it's not just the A-list stories. Since I began writing a weekly column for *The Virginian-Pilot* in January 2007, I've realized that the stories that matter as much to people as the great events of the past are the ones that reside in letters and yearbooks, in boxes in closets and attics of their own homes or live in their memories.

They've shared stories about the hurricane of '33, the old fairgrounds on the bay, the trolleys that ran to Ocean View, the bands that played at the hotels, the ferries that crisscrossed the waterways, the steamships that sailed overnight to Baltimore and New York, the semipro baseball teams that battled for glory, the soldiers and sailors who went off to war. This is the real stuff of our history.

Even though I wrote them at different times over a span of two years, I've rearranged the stories into rough chronological order that runs from the first settlers to the first African American president.

ACKNOWLEDGEMENTS

Hampton Roads is a veritable museum of America's beginnings, and there are many who are its curators and institutions that are its cornerstones. I'm indebted to many of them. For one thing, this book would not exist if the editors of *The Virginian-Pilot*, specifically Denis Finley and Maria Carrillo, had not asked me to write the history column "Our Stories," in which these stories have appeared, or if Nelson Brown had not shepherded them into the newspaper. They also gave permission to reprint staff file photos that went with the stories. Charlie Meads and Kimberly Kent kindly dug many of these images out of storage for me.

I must also thank Louis Guy of the Norfolk Historical Society and Anne Henry of the Princess Anne County/Virginia Beach Historical Society; Norfolk historian Peggy Haile McPhillips; Robert Hitchings and Troy Valos of the Sargeant Memorial Room at the Norfolk Public Library; Mike Cobb of the Hampton History Museum; Stephen Mansfield of Virginia Wesleyan College; Marcus Robbins, naval shipyard historian; Phillip Staten of Riddick's Folly; Lin Olsen of the Great Bridge Battlefield and Waterways History Foundation; George Ramsey of the Virginia Canal Society; the late H.O. Malone of Citizens for a Fort Monroe National Park; Gerri Hollins of the Contraband Historical Society; Linda Jones of Union Mission; Caroline Doonan and Joe Leatherman of the Ocean View Station Museum; Jeff Johnston and Shannon Rickles of the Monitor National Marine Sanctuary; Diane DePew of Colonial National Historical Park; Lillie Gilbert of Wild River Outfitters; author Vickie Shufer; and several parishioners of Kempsville Baptist Church who shared their love of Pleasant Hall.

Many helped with photographs and illustrations: Claudia Jew of the Mariners' Museum; Erin Lopater of the Chrysler Museum of Art; Susan Danforth of the John Carter Brown Library at Brown University; Laura

Waayers of the Naval Historical Foundation; Jim Bradley of the Colonial Williamsburg Foundation; Ben Kunkel of the Decatur House on Lafayette Square; Jon Gorog of the Virginia Maritime Heritage Foundation; Judge William Prince, a descendant of Michael Prince; and Sherry Dewar of TownBank.

Others who shared their stories with me included Barbara Furguson, Gary Fentress, Garland Eaton, Katharine Ashman, Fred Bashara and Elizabeth Clancy.

FIRST LANDING

In the deep woods beside the Chesapeake Bay, residents of the bogs and treetops greet the dawn. Robins skitter on the pine straw floor and peck at bugs concealed therein. There is the half-mad laughter of a pileated woodpecker somewhere in the swamp, the raucous caw of a blackbird, the warbling of a warbler. There's almost a gin-soaked aroma from the pines. As the sun rises in the east, it splashes the green understory of hollies, briars and swamp magnolias with fiery gold.

These are the woods, these are the environs of the Native Americans who were startled by the sudden appearance of Englishmen making their first landing on American soil four centuries ago.

You can walk along what is now Cape Henry Trail at First Landing State Park—where the replica of a small Algonquin Indian village has been erected—continue on the bald cypress and osmanthus trails through Spanish moss–draped woods and be struck dumb with the beauty of the place. And realize what chronicler George Percy meant when he was "almost ravished by the sight thereof."

But he didn't know the half of it, really.

This is land in which, for thousands of years, the sparse population of natives lived in relative harmony with the environment. You get a sense of this by walking the 1.5-mile trail and stepping into the "Chief's House," a sort of lodge that was big enough to accommodate an extended family. It is a simple affair, with saplings lashed together to form the skeleton of the house and support benches. The outside surface is a reed matting that looks like loose elephant skin and smells dank like the woods.

There is a fishing camp with a smaller house and next-door lean-to, a couple of individual family houses and a sweat lodge. This tiny structure was a sort of private sauna where you would sit by a fire, sweat profusely

A Weroan or Great Lorde of Virginia, an Indian chief, with front and back views, engraved in copper by Theodore de Bry. *Courtesy of the John Carter Brown Library, Brown University.*

and then jump in cold water to recharge your batteries. It was healthful, one assumes.

This is all very interesting, built in accordance with what we know about the Late Woodland Period of native life, circa 1600. What is most impressive, though, is the real thing, a circular burial site that contains the remains of sixty-four natives. These were relocated here in 1997, with appropriate ceremony, from nearby acres that were threatened by development. It is appropriately designated "sacred ground."

Those who were here when the colonists arrived were probably successors of the Chesapeake tribe. The Chesapeake had long occupied these lands but enjoyed an uneasy relationship with the powerful empire builder Powhatan. Signage along the trail points out that settlers reported that the Chesapeake were annihilated by tribes loyal to the big chief, although it is likely that women and children weren't killed but rather absorbed by the conquerors.

When the colonists landed, there was a bit of a clash—with only minor wounds—before the natives retreated and the invaders sailed off and settled at Jamestown. But this was the real "first," in the sense that the land here was claimed in the name of the King of England. It wasn't long after that the natives were driven off. Within twenty years, the last of them was gone.

English settlers arrive at Cape Henry in 1607. The beachfront area is now known as First Landing State Park. From a painting by Sidney King. *Courtesy of the National Park Service.*

But looking at the sprawling wooded acres beside the bay, you wonder who the land really belongs to.

As you continue along wooden walkways and leafy paths of the bald cypress trail, there's almost no sign of civilization—except for the occasional jogger huffing by. You can't see them in early spring, but there are certainly cottonmouth snakes and painted turtles in the obsidian waters of the lagoons that sprawl everywhere. At night there must be peepers calling from the banks and owls from the trees.

Cypress trees stand in the swamp, with knobby knees for company. Morning light slants through Spanish moss as if through lace curtains. A far-off woodpecker hammers away and wind murmurs in the treetops.

DROPPING ANCHOR IN THE MIDST OF HISTORY

It seems you can't go anywhere in Hampton Roads without stumbling into a hornet's nest of political intrigue. Take Bennett's Creek in Suffolk, for instance, where my wife and I journeyed by boat from Norfolk on a fall afternoon. We dropped anchor near the Route 17 bridge, rowed ashore for dinner and watched the moon set lazily over the marsh.

Then I looked into the name, which I assumed referred to some fairly recent family; you know, a minor dynasty that settled in the Nansemond region a few generations ago, did some fishing, maybe, and raised a flock of kids. But a fascinating picture emerges. Like just about every place name in this history-besotted region, Bennett goes back and back and back. And his story? Well, it involves radical Puritans in England, the beheading of a king, a governorship, a religious conversion and, at last, an act of charity.

Richard Bennett was the leader of a group of Puritans who settled along the Nansemond River in 1635 after the Indians of the same name had been run off. Having brought forty others with him, he was awarded two thousand acres of land—fifty acres per settler. Along with his brother, Phillip, and his cousin, Robert, Richard took control of over one thousand waterfront acres near what was to become Bennett's Landing at the intersection of the Nansemond and Bennett's Creek. Under the same acts authorizing Norfolk and other cities around here, Nansemond Town was to be born there, but it didn't take.

What did take, though, was a hotbed of dissenters from the official Church of England, which held sway over the fledgling American colonies.

Bennett and about seventy of his neighbors petitioned church elders in Boston to send some ministers, fast, to keep them on the straight and narrow. The petitioners, according to the elders, "bewail their sad condition for the want of means of salvation."

Bennett's Creek. The author's boat anchored overnight in Bennett's Creek just off the entrance to the Nansemond River. The river is named for a Puritan leader who settled nearby in 1635.

A couple of frocked fellows did make it to these shores and began preaching and going door to door exhorting, if not haranguing, the locals to hear the words of the Lord. But instead the word reached Jamestown, and the thin-skinned Governor Berkeley persuaded the House of Burgesses to declare, "For the preservation of the purity of doctrine and unity of the church, all ministers whatsoever who shall reside in the colony, are to be conformed to the orders and constitution of the Church of England." If these nonconformists continued to preach, either publicly or privately, they would be compelled to depart "with all convenience." They high-tailed it out pretty quickly. Furthermore, Bennett and many of his followers went into exile in Maryland.

It gets better.

Over in merry olde England, Oliver Cromwell, a right-wing Puritan zealot, slaughtered several thousand Irish Catholics, toppled Charles I from the throne and had him decapitated, establishing a Parliament-run Commonwealth of England. "Roundheads," some of them were called, after their tendency to eschew once fashionable curls in favor of what amounted to seventeenth-century buzz cuts.

Cromwell was not about to put up with troublesome royalists—Cavaliers—in Virginia, so he sent a fleet of warships to put them down. A quick settlement followed, with Berkeley stepping down and none other than Richard Bennett becoming the first governor of the commonwealth of Virginia. Bennett held sway in Jamestown from 1652 to 1655.

After Cromwell died of malaria and kidney stones—he was so hated that his body was exhumed, hanged, decimated and decapitated!—Berkeley came back into power. This time, Bennett wasn't run out of town. He became the agent for the Virginia colony in England and major general of the Virginia militia.

But he wasn't finished with irritating Berkeley. When Quaker leader George Fox traveled through Nansemond County in 1672, Bennett and many others fell under his spell. The Quakers refused to obey religious laws and some of their followers were expelled from the House of Burgesses for their "wayward" views. Berkeley called Bennett's band "unreasonable and turbulent."

Bennett died in 1675 and was buried at his homeplace near Driver. Among his descendants were several Virginian heavy hitters, including John Randolph ("I am an aristocrat") and Robert E. Lee. His will left three hundred acres to Nansemond County and stipulated that rents from the land be given to aged or underprivileged persons.

You never know what you're going to find, especially in early Virginia.

BURNING AMBITION

The reopening of the Naval Shipyard Museum, with its new exhibit on Portsmouth and Gosport, got me thinking about how it all happened. It was the burning ambition of a wealthy Scottish merchant, Andrew Sprowle, that launched the original shipyard and sparked the growth of the city. But it was the same ambition that also led to his miserable demise in the company of those he befriended.

Sprowle, who had made his way to Norfolk County in the 1730s, saw his opportunity when his friend William Crawford began selling waterfront lots in the new village named after the great English port city, Portsmouth. As his fortunes grew, he expended southward to undeveloped land, where he was able to start a shipyard.

What drove Sprowle was the unquenchable thirst of the British navy for shipbuilding and ship-repairing facilities in the colonies. Knowing that he would get the attention of British ship captains, he named the new yard, and the town that grew up around it, Gosport (read that "God's port) after a similar installation next to the great English port.

And prosper he did. The shipyard, the largest in the colonies, consisted of a ninety-one-foot, five-story warehouse with hand-hewn stone stairs brought from England, a giant crane with brass wheels and pulleys and several other buildings. He lived grandly in a three-story house with stone chimneys and an expansive balcony overlooking the Elizabeth River. He became trustee of the new Portsmouth town, vestry member of Trinity Church and a leading merchant.

An interesting item appears in the September 22, 1768 *Virginia Gazette*, a notice about a runaway eighteen-year-old slave named Solomon, a blacksmith. "Whoever brings him to Gosport shall have 40 s. reward," the ad promises. It is signed Andrew Sprowle.

The Gosport Navy Yard, founded in the 1730s by Andrew Sprowle, an ardent Tory. *Courtesy of Marcus W. Robbins.*

Things continued swimmingly after the arrival of a fellow Scot, John Murray, Lord Dunmore, in 1771. Sprowle often entertained the then popular Virginia governor. But the puffed-up, heavy-handed Dunmore began to lose favor as he overreacted to the stirrings of independence in Williamsburg. When Dunmore retreated from the capital in the spring of 1775, he took refuge at Gosport. He and his retinue moved into Sprowle's mansion and his troops were quartered at a shipyard warehouse.

So Portsmouth's little next-door neighbor, Gosport, briefly served as the colonial capital of Virginia, and Dunmore referred to Sprowle as its "lieutenant governor." Some reports say that Sprowle entertained Dunmore lavishly during that period, but a memorandum from his feisty wife, Kate, shows the opposite. The royal governor and his staff descended on their house, provisions and effects, "rioted in them for five months" and "practiced all manner of barbarous treatment" toward them, she claimed.

Things started getting dicey as Dunmore's fortunes sank and reinforcements failed to arrive. A letter from Sprowle published in the December 29 *Gazette* indicates that he watched daily for the arrival of British warships. "God send them soon. While the soldiers remains [*sic*] at Gosport, I am safe."

It seemed that the bed Sprowle had chosen to lie on was getting downright prickly. Dunmore had just suffered a humiliating defeat at Great Bridge and fled to the safety of his ships in Norfolk Harbor. On New Year's Day 1776, he retaliated by opening fire on Norfolk and setting fire to waterfront warehouses. Dunmore would continue to visit havoc on Hampton Roads cities for several months, and there is no doubt that Sprowle was one of those who kept his ships provisioned. The Patriots seized the shipyard and demolished his home.

Finally, in May 1776, Dunmore weighed anchor and, along with many of the Loyalists, including Sprowle and his family, sailed up the Chesapeake Bay and landed at Gwynn's Island near the Rappahannock River. Sprowle, no longer useful to Dunmore, was, according to one account, savagely abused by the soldiers. It isn't clear how he met his end, whether from beatings, an outbreak of smallpox or several battles with the Patriots that followed, but the loyal Scotsman ended up in a shallow grave on the island as Dunmore sailed away.

The Gosport shipyard, destroyed and rebuilt several times, became one of the great naval facilities in the world. But its beginnings were clouded by one man's inability to extricate himself from the grip of his self-interest.

ON THE EDGE OF OUR HISTORY

It's such an unexpected encounter. Driving along Potters Road at the northern edge of Ocean Naval Air Station, you come upon a sign for "Upper Wolfsnare" and a long country lane that bumps over abandoned railroad tracks, ending at a white, two-story home in the style of an English manor house. Three acres surround the house, with a magnificent swamp chestnut oak on one side that must be older than the bones of Thomas Walke III, the man who built the place in 1759. Maybe it is as old as his grandfather who settled in Lynnhaven Parish from Barbados more than one hundred years before.

Upper Wolfsnare, so called because of its location on the upper reaches of Wolf Snare Creek, is owned by the Princess Anne County/Virginia Beach Historic Society. It's so odd having this place here. Smack dab in the middle of the high-decibel corridor near the air station, you wonder how it was ever preserved. In fact, the state planned to knock it down and dig up the property to use the earth for expressway ramps, but preservationists saved it and deeded it over to the society. And here it stands, begging to tell its story.

First, the house: inside, there's a wide passageway instead of the kind of center hall you'd expect. The drawing room on the right is dominated by dark, hand-carved wainscoting. You can see through cracks between the random-width heart pine floorboards. On one wall is a portrait of one of the Walkes, perhaps one of many cousins. Absent is any likeness of Thomas Walke IV, the son of the builder who went to Richmond in the spring of 1788 and helped Virginia, by a narrow margin, ratify the U.S. Constitution. The room on the left (chair railing, with molding) has a copy of a painting of a grand reception given by Martha Washington. She and George were married in 1759, the year the house was built.

Anne Henry, a historical society member and avid local historian, gave me a tour—it's only open to the public on Wednesdays in July and August,

Upper Wolfsnare, built by Thomas Walke III in 1759. *Courtesy of the Princess Anne County/Virginia Beach Historical Society.*

so she arranged with the caretakers to let me see it. "I think it clearly shows what one segment of life was like in the eighteenth century," she says. "It was a major piece of our history."

And so it is, but there's another side of the story, and it begins in Barbados. The original Thomas Walke came to Virginia in 1662 from that British-ruled Caribbean island and soon began shipping goods back and forth between the new American colony and Barbados, where his family remained. In the hold of his small fleet of ships, he may have included slaves.

A new book (2007) by historian April Lee Hatfield, *Atlantic Virginia: Intercolonial Relations in the Seventeenth Century*, delves deeply into Walke's Barbados connections. Hatfield writes that Walke developed close ties with William Byrd I, one of Virginia's elite planters and traders. "Many Virginians interested in Barbados trade sought African slaves from the island," she writes. Barbados also "likely provided Byrd with a market for Indian slaves he acquired in exchange for Barbadian rum." What human misery this route must have known!

According to the official Virginia Beach website, when Thomas Walke III died in 1761—just two years after building this house—he left to his infant son seven thousand acres and fifty-five slaves.

And then there's this. In the Papers of James Madison, available online, you can find a little-known episode involving Thomas Walke. In April 1783, he petitioned Virginia's delegates to Congress—that's what they were called then—for the right "to reclaim our slaves that were wrested from us by the British enimy [*sic*]." It would be, he said, "a glaring piece of injustice" if they were not given that right. He further complained that "several hundred of the above slaves sailed during the last week to Nova Scotia."

You might wonder if some of those no doubt scared, but now free, individuals fled from this fascinating place out on the edge of our history.

THE BRITISH ARE COMING!

What strikes you first as you pass through the entrance is the thickness of the walls, two feet deep at least, and then the wide heart pine floorboards and wavy glass windows blurring the passing traffic on Princess Anne Road. In the front parlor, with its elaborate crown molding and powder blue walls, a glass cabinet displays artifacts found on the property: musket balls, cannon shot, clay pipe stems, pottery shards and, most fascinating of all, George III British coins.

The history of this place comes roaring back with the flash of gunpowder, the urgency of shouted commands. This is Pleasant Hall, one of the most historically significant buildings in Hampton Roads, a place that watched over—and perhaps played a part in—a small but crucial battle as the American Revolutionary War began.

Just imagine this fellow, John Murray, fourth earl of Dunmore, outsmarted and embarrassed by Patrick Henry and other upstarts, forced into exile in Gosport, where he watched the trappings of government power fall away. And then consider the reports he heard about a stash of gunpowder hidden at a place called Kemp's Landing. It was time, he blustered, to "reduce this colony to a proper sense of their duty."

Leading a force of British Regulars and Loyalists, Lord Dunmore marched toward Kempe's Landing, later Kempsville. The locals knew he was coming, lore has it, because of an elegant rogue named Peter Singleton. The young officer, as extravagant in dress as he was reckless at cards, supposedly rode into town from Great Bridge, Paul Revere style, to warn that the British were coming! By land!

So it was that local minutemen hid the gunpowder and then, with hearts surely in their throats, stood up to the British on the night of November 16, 1775.

Pleasant Hall. This photo was taken about 1972. *Courtesy of the National Register of Historic Places.*

"They fired one gun at our flanking partee and two at our advance Guard," one British soldier wrote. "This was returned by a heavy fire from the Grandeers, which instantly put the villains to flight." One Patriot, John Ackiss, became the first southerner killed in the Revolutionary War. Two others were taken prisoner.

The Skirmish at Kempsville, as it became known, was quickly over and Dunmore immediately demanded that everyone in town take a loyalty oath. Those who "could not conveniently run away," as one writer put it, took the oath at once and swallowed bitterly as red cloth badges were pinned to their breasts.

Dunmore set up temporary headquarters at the home of George Logan, a Scotch Tory. He had never seen a finer house in Virginia, he was to write. He dined there and held a lavish victory party. Then, still puffed up with victory, he foolishly marched his troops into slaughter against Patriots waiting for him at Great Bridge.

But as far as Logan's house goes, does it still exist?

The official story is that Pleasant Hall, built in 1769, is the one Logan built. But if you look up the 1972 application by Virginia Beach to have the house listed on the National Register of Historic Places, you find a different story. Judging from an inscription chiseled in a brick beside a basement window, the house was built in 1779, likely by none other than Peter Singleton.

Kempe's Landing, a sketch by Emily Whaley. *Courtesy of the Local History Collection, Virginia Wesleyan College.*

A slightly different view stems from historic research by John H. Robertson of Chesapeake. He found that the house was built by Samuel Tennant, a ship's captain, around 1765, and was soon after sold to Singleton. Further, he concluded, Logan's house was on the west side of what is known as Overland Road, where Pleasant Hall's present owner, Kempsville Baptist Church, now sits.

Three women from the church, Elizabeth McBride, Marjorie Stanton and Edna Stocks, showed me through the house. Then we went out front and discovered the supposedly definitive brick beside a basement window. But the date "April 1771" is only faintly scratched on the surface, not chiseled, and could have been added later.

It isn't clear that we'll ever know the truth; for now, at least, we get to choose.

Hmm, which version seems best, the one about the disgraced Tory or the dashing Patriot?

A BROKEN HEART

Visiting the Moses Myers House in downtown Norfolk is like finding yourself in another century. The ceilings, fireplace mantels, paintings, furnishings, dishes, musical instruments—almost everything is authentic, right down to the Spode China, the bed warmers and the sheet music.

We know part of the story of this remarkable fellow. Arriving in the spring of 1787—over 220 years ago—he quickly became the first successful Jewish merchant in the city, an importer with a fleet of ships, a patron of the arts and sire of a political and professional dynasty.

It was no accident that he and his wife, Eliza, chose Norfolk. He knew that he could make money here because of the city's deep-water port and the state's liberal money policies. But it is the little-known beginning and end of Myers's career that reveal the most about his life, showing him to be both incredibly gutsy and terribly vulnerable.

Immediately after the outbreak of the war in 1775, Myers enlisted in a New York company of the Continental army. But he wasn't much at soldiering and found a far more useful way to contribute to the cause. With the fall of New York to the British, he began secretly importing military supplies into the colonies from France and the Netherlands. His father was Dutch and they had many contacts in Amsterdam.

According to a fascinating unpublished biography by Thomas Costa and Peter Stewart—which I read in the basement library of the Myers House—the twenty-four-year-old Myers soon found himself in St. Eustatius, a tiny Dutch Caribbean island that had become a hub of the risky, but lucrative, arms trade with the rebellious colonies. This audacious enterprise, one British admiral declared, "had done England more harm than all of the arms of her most potent enemies, and alone supported the infamous American rebellion."

This page: Moses and Eliza Myers, oil on poplar, portraits by Gilbert Stuart. Moses Myers, who owned a fleet of ships, was Norfolk's first successful Jewish merchant. *Courtesy of the Chrysler Museum of Art.*

The British had had enough of this. They declared war on the Netherlands and, in February 1781, sent a fleet of warships to the island, which quickly surrendered. Virtually all of its shippers, including Myers, were taken prisoner, sent to England and locked up. All of the possessions of the company that he had helped form were seized.

The Revolution was soon over, however, and Myers returned to New York. He began the exhausting ordeal of collecting debts owed to his company and managed to crawl out of debt. The good part was that the enterprising trader had established a vast network of contacts around the world.

It didn't seem to bother him that Norfolk, after being torched by the British, had not yet recovered, that its water was filthy, its streets muddy and its overall health deplorable. There were so many burned-out homes and businesses that it was sometimes called "Chimney Town." He saw nothing but potential.

"I like the place and its inhabitants," Myers wrote to a friend in June 1787. "I shall find no difficulty in getting a house, and I think from appearances we shall do well."

And they did. He and Eliza entertained grandly at their house on Freemason Street. The streets echoed with the sound of their horses and carriage. He owned warehouses and several ships and speculated in banks, canal projects and steamboat lines. She bore him a dozen children.

His problem, though, was that most of his money was tied up in shipping ventures, and when hostilities began to break out, first between Britain and France and then between Britain and the United States, embargoes virtually shut down shipping. The War of 1812 and the disruptions that followed were devastating. By 1819, with the nation in financial panic, two of his sons were forced into bankruptcy, and their father, attempting to shield them, followed. He narrowly avoided imprisonment and losing his house.

"My heart bleeds when I reflect on my situation and that of my family," he wrote in October 1819. He would spend much of the rest of his life trying to rebuild his fortune. Sadly, before he died in 1835, Eliza and six of their nine surviving children died from various illnesses, including yellow fever. It was said of Myers that he died of a broken heart.

THE HORRORS OF WAR

In the bitter wind of a winter Sunday afternoon, as rifles and muskets boomed and gun smoke filled the air, men and boys in red coats fell in a heap on the cold ground.

You can imagine, but only in part, what the real scene must have been like as the cream of Britain's army, the grenadiers, marched shoulder to shoulder into the savage gunfire that awaited them on another December day at Great Bridge.

Why wouldn't those Rebels, mostly unseasoned volunteers, turn and run at the sight of professional soldiers, as Lord Dunmore had predicted? Instead, the Patriots stood their ground and waited until the redcoats were fifty yards away, then mowed them down, almost to a man. The Battle of Great Bridge was one of the most one-sided contests in the Revolutionary War, with between 60 and 102 British soldiers killed or wounded, while a single American, a captain, suffered a slight wound to his thumb. It was also one of the most pivotal, causing Dunmore to pull up stakes and leave Virginia for good.

Now, annually, the Chesapeake Parks and Recreation Department sponsors Battle of Great Bridge observances, reenacting the confrontation that occurred on the frosty morning of December 9, 1775.

In December 2008, there were about sixty reenactors, more or less equally divided between British and Patriot fighters. A genial Bill Blair of Gloucester played Colonel William Woolford, who led the Americans, and a dour, black-hatted David Pondolfino of Williamsburg portrayed Dunmore. The men make their own costumes, sometimes switching allegiances, depending on the number on each side. They own their muskets or rifles and roll their own black powder cartridges. And, yes, they make a lot of noise and smoke. As Blair said in narrating the event, you don't expect reenactors to stand in the cold all day without blasting away at one another.

Redcoats blast away at Patriots in a December reenactment of the Battle of Great Bridge.
Courtesy of Nancie Laing.

Considering the weather, there was a good turnout. Tents and exhibits were manned by the Norfolk County Historical Society, the Daughters of the American Revolution and others, as well as a few craftspeople. The Great Bridge Battlefield and Waterways History Foundation, which has an office near the site, made sure that the contenders did not have to fall and die, twice each day, without the blessing of cookies and hot chocolate. Children were impressed by the pretend soldiers, especially their booming guns. And the guns did boom on that far-off December day.

Dunmore had been flush with victory from a skirmish at Kempsville a few weeks before and decided to show the Patriot cowards a thing or two. Great Bridge, the little community at the Virginia–North Carolina crossroads, was vital to controlling goods flowing to and from Norfolk. He had built a ramshackle fort there. It was dubbed "the pig pen" by the Patriots, but it was fortified by four-pounder cannon that effectively guarded the causeway.

Prompted by George Washington, who felt that the fate of the Revolution depended on forcing Dunmore out of Norfolk, regiments of minutemen from around the region marched to Great Bridge. Among the contingent from Culpeper was a twenty-year-old lieutenant named John Marshall, who was destined to become the most influential chief justice in the history of the Supreme Court.

The Patriots built redoubts and for several days exchanged gunfire with Dunmore's forces but, because of the cannon, declined to attack. Fortunately, the British made the first move, marching six abreast across a narrow causeway just north of the present Great Bridge.

The British were mostly using smoothbore muskets, which are not as accurate as the rifled American guns, and the gunners' aim was true. The genteel Captain Charles Fordyce, leading about 60 grenadiers and 120 others, fell within fifteen feet of the breastworks, his body riddled with no fewer than fourteen bullets.

One witness told of "a vast effusion of blood, so dreadful that it beggars description, a scene that, when the dead and wounded were bro't off, was too much. I then saw the horrors of war in perfection, worse than can be imagin'd; 10 and 12 bullets thro' many; limbs broke in 2 or 3 places; brains turning out. Good God, what a sight!"

Sunday, after lying on the cold ground for what seemed an eternity, these vanquished soldiers sprang to their feet and went off, perhaps in search of hot chocolate.

THUNDERBOLTS OF JUPITER

It was a good day for a walk. Sunny, windy, cool, with a dull tidewater blush of color in the trees. On the York River, whitecaps and white sails speckled the water. And out on the fields surrounding the historic village of Yorktown, flags indicating where siege lines had once formed snapped in the breeze.

And I couldn't help but think of that time, 227 years ago, when the terrible fury had been unleashed against the defenders of Yorktown by American and French forces. Eight days of relentless, round-the-clock bombardment pulverized British defenses and rained death and misery upon them. Then, finally, a white flag flew and the world was turned upside down.

In 2008, the folks at Colonial National Historical Park and the Yorktown Victory Center observed Yorktown Day, the anniversary of the British surrender. One of the highlights was a parade at 1:30 p.m., but there was much more: tours and demonstrations, musket and artillery drills, encampments and hands-on interpretive programs. Like me, you may have done this a number of times, but the miracle of this place always delivers. Especially at this time of year.

Out on the bluffs overlooking the river there's an array of cannon, the largest of which is a twenty-four-pounder. As an interpreter will tell you, George Washington and his French allies were able to stand off, out of range of the defenders' six- and twelve-pound guns, and wreak havoc upon the town. There's another fearsome weapon, a mortar that fired shells that burst in the air above the fortifications. The inscription on one of the ancient mortars facing the harbor is in Latin, but a translation is provided: "Send not the rays of the sun but the thunderbolts of Jupiter."

It had come to this: British general Cornwallis, after leaving Portsmouth, had chosen Yorktown for its harbor and, he thought, defensible location. But he hadn't reckoned on a French blockade of the Chesapeake Bay or on the ability of the American and French forces to march from New York, haul

The surrender of Cornwallis after a long and punishing siege, painting by Trumbull. *Courtesy of the National Archives.*

their big guns down the bay on ships and place him and his men in a perfect hellhole of destruction.

During the bombardment, most of the once prosperous town was leveled, including the house belonging to former colonial secretary Thomas Nelson that Cornwallis used as headquarters. All that's left are the stones of the original foundations.

Down on the waterfront, you can get an idea of how devastating the attack was. Near a picnic area are the remains of a cave carved out of sandstone. You can peer in and just about hear the cries of children. This is where townsfolk, their homes destroyed, sought shelter. Or, when it reopens—there's construction going on to repair a footbridge—you can hike up a former tobacco road where a sign informs you that, after Nelson's home came under fire, Cornwallis and his staff built a kind of grotto where they hid while their defenses crumbled and their troops were slaughtered.

At one point, the British made a desperate nighttime attempt to flee across the York, only to be hurled back by a sudden storm. The last hope was gone. The defenders were staring at heavy guns now brought to within point-blank range. Cornwallis realized that, as far as his troops were concerned, it would be "wanton and inhuman" to continue.

The bombardment was still in progress on the chilly morning of October 17 when a lone drummer boy, his heart no doubt thumping, stepped upon the parapet and began an unsteady cadence and an officer holding high a white flag fell in with him. American and French guns finally fell silent. Two days later, the vanquished defenders, Englishmen, Scotsmen, Welchmen, Hessians and Loyalists, marched out to what is now called Surrender Field and, bitterly, gave up their weapons.

It was British Prime Minister Frederick North who put the coda on the American Revolution when he heard the news: "Oh God! It's all over!"

AT CAPE HENRY,
A GUIDING LIGHT

One, two, three, four, five...
If you climb to the top of the Old Cape Henry Lighthouse, that's just the beginning, merely steps leading to the greeting station. There will be 189 more, at least by my count, including those going up to the base of the tower. You pause at the base, catching your breath, walking slowly around and gazing up at the red stone octagon rising in the humid morning sky. Then it hits you: you're looking at history.

This isn't the oldest still-standing lighthouse in America. That honor goes the light at Sandy Hook, New Jersey, built in 1764. Nor is it the tallest (Cape Hatteras). But it was a great leap of faith for the new republic, its first public works project.

The Cape Henry Light, a long-sought beacon for guiding ships safely past the Virginia Capes, had a troubled beginning. It was first authorized by the colonial General Assembly in 1752, to be paid for with tobacco revenue, but Britain disallowed the project. Two decades later, the colonists tried again, actually beginning construction with sandstone hauled from quarries in Northern Virginia. But this time, the Revolutionary War interfered. During the war, signal fires were used to warn of the approach of enemy ships. At last, with victory achieved and the new government in place, Congress, with the backing of George Washington, approved the project in 1789.

Washington also picked John McComb Jr., who had designed Government House in New York as the first presidential residence, as the builder. Using the sandstone blocks that had been hauled there before the war, McComb set about his task. He had to dig down twenty feet before he could find solid ground on which to build the foundation. You can see the base, rising from the sandy earth, but then the beautiful blocks of redstone, giving the light its distinctive character, begin.

A Guiding Light at Cape Henry, photo by Charlie Meads. *Courtesy of* The Virginian-Pilot.

You scratch your head. How could they have done this? A perfect octagon rising ninety feet above the ground to the glass-enclosed lantern above. You enter the eleven-foot-thick base, lined with whitewashed brick, and look up. The spiral steel staircase seems to form a perfect nautilus shape as it rises.

One, two, three…Your heart begins to thud, eighty-four stairs (I think), then two steep ladders (eighteen more steps) and you're there. "We made it!" a few others say as they gain the lantern room and look out at the best view they've ever had of the Virginia coast.

Turning slowly, you can see tourist hotels and high-rise condos near Lynnhaven Bay, Town Center, the Virginia Beach Oceanfront and then the vast Atlantic. Coal ships ride at anchor near the capes. A squadron of pelicans glides just above the gentle surf, and just beyond the breakers, dolphins rise and fall. And of course, the new black-and-white steel lighthouse, a mere baby at 127 years old, bisects the view.

The old light did its job for just about ninety years, guiding what must have been hundreds of thousands of ships into safe harbor. There was a brief interruption during the Civil War after Confederate troops disabled the light. A lightship stationed between the capes took over until it could be repaired.

The latest beach fashion, 1896 at Virginia Beach. *Courtesy of* The Virginian-Pilot.

But it still stands, the official symbol of the city of Virginia Beach. How lucky can we get—not just one but two historic lighthouses. It has been faithfully maintained since 1930 by the Association for the Preservation of Virginia Antiquities. Some sixty thousand visitors see it annually, most tromping up these ancient stairs. The APVA has kept the memories, if not the light, burning.

THE UNLUCKIEST SHIP

I f ever there was a star-crossed ship, it was the *Chesapeake*. The thirty-eight-gun frigate, built at the Gosport Navy Yard in Portsmouth, was shorter, beamier and slower than its famous sisters *Constitution* and *Constellation*. An odd duck, really, foreshortened because the scarce oak was diverted for the other ships.

And unlucky.

The last of the six warships that gave birth to the U.S. Navy, the *Chesapeake* suffered from delays and disputes among builders and naval architects. Finally, after being fitted out near Hampton, the vessel stood out into Hampton Roads on a clear Monday morning, June 22, 1807, and set sail for the Mediterranean to relieve the *Constitution*. A gentle southwest breeze filled square-rigged sails.

Lying at anchor in Lynnhaven Bay was a squadron of British ships —nothing to worry about, the officers of the *Chesapeake* thought as they steered east into the Atlantic. The United States was still on friendly terms with its former mother country, although there was one issue that rankled both sides—deserters. Many sailors of the Royal Navy had gone missing, and there was reason to believe that some of them were then and there on the *Chesapeake*.

One of the ships from the squadron, HMS *Leopard*, had also set sail and, several miles off the coast, sent a boarding party to the American ship and demanded the right to muster and inspect the crew. When Commodore James Barron refused, the *Leopard* fired a warning shot and prepared to attack.

The problem was that the *Chesapeake* was in no position to fight. Rushed into leaving, its decks were still cluttered with lumber, casks of wine, furniture and baggage. The gun deck was worse—a junkyard of anchor cables, hammocks and various other hindrances. Not a single gun was primed and ready, and when the drums beat to battle stations, "chaos reigned aboard the *Chesapeake*," according to a book, *Six Frigates, the Epic History of the founding of the U.S. Navy*, by Ian W. Toll.

> *At 4:30 p.m., the* Leopard *opened fire on the* Chesapeake *from pistol-shot range. Most of the balls struck* Chesapeake *amidships, creating secondary explosions of splinters on the interior walls of the bulwarks and gun deck. A few crashed through the rigging, sending down a rain of cordage and fragments of spars.*

By the second and third broadsides, the *Chesapeake* lay in ruins, able to fire only one gun, for honor's sake. Four crew members lay dead or dying and seventeen others were wounded. Barron had no choice but to send up the white flag of surrender. It was both a humiliating and infuriating loss. Angry crowds crowded Norfolk and Portsmouth wharves when the battered ship limped home, and the nation nearly went to war with Britain then and there, rather than five years later.

Junior officers on the *Chesapeake* felt that they had "disgraced [themselves]." Barron was court-martialed and found guilty of "neglecting to clear his

The British warship *Leopard* devastated the *Chesapeake*, one of America's first frigates, in an incident that almost led to war in 1807. *Courtesy of the Mariners' Museum.*

ship for action." Several duels were fought over the loss, including one years later in which an insulted Barron shot and killed American naval hero Stephen Decatur.

The *Chesapeake* had one chance at redemption six years later. Under the command of James Lawrence, the ship sailed out of Boston Harbor and challenged the British warship *Shannon*. On June 1, 1813, the two exchanged savage gunfire, but the *Shannon* got the better of the argument. Of the 150 men stationed on the quarter deck, 100 were killed or wounded, including nearly all of the American officers. Wounded and bleeding to death, Lawrence cried out, famously, "Don't give up the ship!"

But in fact there was no choice by then other than surrender. The *Chesapeake* was taken as a prize of war and eventually broken up to make houses and a mill—the Chesapeake Mill—in Wickham, England.

There's a model of the *Chesapeake* and an exhibit that illustrates both battles at the Hampton Roads Naval Museum at Nauticus. The display case for the model includes a piece of wood that was removed from the mill and returned to America in 1996.

OUR COUNTRY, RIGHT OR WRONG?

At a banquet at the Exchange Hotel in Norfolk in April 1816, no doubt flush with wine and victory, naval officers and local officials raised their glasses to the daring hero of Tripoli and the War of 1812, Stephen Decatur. And Decatur, not given to modesty, probably got a little carried away.

"Our country!" he toasted. "In her intercourse with foreign nations, may she always be in the right; but our country, right or wrong!"

This line, often misquoted as "my country, right or wrong," has long been held up as an example of over-exuberant patriotism. Nevertheless, in the heady days following America's first demonstration of real naval power, you can imagine the ovation he must have received.

If you look up the quote, you find it has been famously elaborated upon. Half a century later, Carl Schurz, German-born general and U.S. senator, put it this way: "Our country right or wrong. When right, to be kept right; when wrong, to be put right." British author G.K. Chesterton later scoffed, "'My country right or wrong' is a thing no patriot would think of saying except in a desperate case. It is like saying, 'My mother, drunk or sober.'"

Decatur, who married Susan Wheeler, daughter of Norfolk mayor Luke Wheeler, moved to Washington and built a mansion on Lafayette Square. But wait, there's a Portsmouth connection, a sad one, that tells the rest of the story.

In the churchyard of Trinity Church are dozens of faded gravestones, most of them rather modest, even though they belong to Patriots of the Revolutionary War. But right next to the church's parish hall is a rather imposing grave on a raised slab, surrounded by an iron fence and decorated by a plaque that reads, "Commodore James Barron, U.S.N. Senior officer aboard the Frigate *Chesapeake*. Placed by Fort Norfolk Chapter U.S. Daughters of 1812." Next to the grave are the tiny markers of two infant grandchildren.

Naval hero Stephen Decatur strikes a swashbuckling pose. *Courtesy of the Naval Historical Foundation.*

It was Barron who, upon encountering the British ship *Leopard* more than two hundred years ago, gave up the *Chesapeake* without a fight and years later killed Decatur in a duel over a supposed slight. He had been suspended after the *Chesapeake* affair but returned to duty and became superintendent of Gosport Navy Yard. At the time of his death in 1851, he was the highest-ranking officer in the navy.

Historians note that Barron may have been a scapegoat because the navy had ordered him to take his ill-prepared ship to sea. And an apparent last-minute effort to avoid the duel was thwarted by others who had it in for Decatur. But Decatur's death is his legacy.

A portrait of Barron, made in 1829, hangs in the Norfolk History Museum at the Willoughby-Baylor House. You can't help but observe a baleful look in his blue eyes and a touch of biliousness, either from a full life or an occasional whiskey that helped drown his sorrows. Next to the painting is a case with a pair of dueling pistols made by "D. Egg," gun maker to the prince of Wales, in 1810. There is speculation that John Myers, eldest son of Moses Myers, loaned them to Barron and that one of them may have fired the fatal shot.

A somewhat whimsical coda to the Barron story is that right next to the churchyard on High Street is a beautiful art deco theater. Opened in 1945, it hosted community stage presentations for thirty years. Then, after a hiatus of twelve years, it was rescued and reopened in its present grandeur as a cinema-eatery. It is and always has been the Commodore Theater, named for the fellow who rests so near.

SMITTEN

H e was dashing, rich and famous. She was beautiful, high-spirited and talented. And determined to meet him.

When Stephen Decatur's frigate *Congress* anchored in Hampton Roads in November 1805, the mayor of Norfolk, Luke Wheeler, a rich merchant and doting father, organized a boating party in the hopes of visiting the ship. They set out for the Roads, came alongside and got permission to board the impressive vessel.

Decatur was already ashore with his guest, the ambassador from Tunisia, but that was only a temporary setback. While others toured the ship, Susan Wheeler, the mayor's daughter, slipped into the captain's stateroom, where she discovered a miniature portrait of Decatur. So this was the hero of the Barbary wars, the new nation's most eligible bachelor!

The next day, at a properly lavish dinner for Decatur and the diplomat, the mayor's daughter managed to get an introduction. The young captain, just recently promoted as a result of his exploits, was quickly undone. "The attraction of Stephen Decatur and Susan Wheeler was overwhelming," writes Frederick C. Leiner in a new book, *The End of Barbary Terror*.

She was "slim, fashionable, and vivacious," Leiner adds, a drawing room sophisticate who played the harp and sang, who was conversant in French and Italian and held her own in polite conversation with ambassadors and statesmen. She also knew how to ask the right questions, tactfully inquiring of an aide to Decatur whether the ceremonial sword he had been awarded by Congress was meant for a certain lady friend in Philadelphia. It wasn't.

There was a certain mystery about her. James Tertius de Kay, in a 2004 book, *Rage for Glory, the Life of Commodore Stephen Decatur, USN*, says there were rumors "that she was Wheeler's illegitimate child, and had been born in the obscurity of Elk Ridge Landing, Maryland, where her father ran an

Decatur and Susan Wheeler, daughter of the mayor of Norfolk, were clearly smitten with each other at their first meeting. *Courtesy of the Decatur House on Lafayette Square.*

ironworks." Nothing is known of her mother, he writes, "but it was whispered that she had been a mulatto."

More intriguing was the list of suitors she had rejected, including the notoriously lecherous Aaron Burr, then vice president, and Jerome Bonaparte, brother of Napoleon. While the latter's frigate was in Hampton Roads, the Frenchman couldn't keep his eyes off her and impulsively asked for her hand in marriage.

But no one was as smitten as Decatur, and there began a whirlwind courtship—including the abrupt end of the Philadelphia romance. Knowing of her talents as a musician, Decatur sent Susan a gift of sheet music. When he returned to Norfolk in January, the two headstrong lovers, as de Kay terms them, fell into each other's arms. They were married on March 8 by the Reverend Benjamin Porter Grigsby of the Norfolk Presbyterian congregation.

The couple moved to Washington and, with the wealth he had amassed from ship-captured prize money, bought a lot across from the White House, hired noted architect Benjamin Henry Latrobe and had a luxurious mansion erected. It was designed specifically for entertainment, allowing for the comings and goings of servants and musicians.

But marriage to a naval hero who spent many months at sea and seemed heedless of his safety was nerve-wracking. In February 1815, Susan wrote to the secretary of the navy, asking that her husband not be sent to the Mediterranean again. She was "so horrifi'd and perturb'd during the last two or three years," she wrote, and could not bear another separation. It didn't work, and Decatur was soon off again. But he wrote to her, urging, "Do not be anxious about me, my beloved. I shall soon press you to my heart."

And he did. Sadly, they lived only fourteen months in the Decatur House, now a museum on Lafayette Square. Her husband was cut down not in a firefight at sea but in a petty duel with a former associate, Commodore James Barron of Hampton. Susan was inconsolable, a "total wreck," she admitted. Although he left her $75,000, a fortune then, she frittered away most of the money and had to sell the mansion.

Susan had a lifelong interest in religion and converted to Catholicism. When Congress awarded her $7,000 for her husband's service, she donated all of it to Georgetown College. She lived out her life in a cottage on the campus and was buried nearby. But as the growing university began to expand, she was twice disinterred and, finally, moved to lie at the foot of Stephen's tomb in Philadelphia. "Reunited, a Naval Hero and his Belle," was the headline in the *Philadelphia Inquirer*.

WITHERING FIRE

I magine a hazy dawn 195 years ago, mid-tide, an armada of twenty barges loaded with an overwhelming force of British sailors and marines approaches. Their target is fifty acres of sand and scrub pines at the mouth of the Elizabeth River known as Craney Island. A merchant sea captain by the name of Arthur Emmerson, once thought to be a natural successor to his father as a man of the cloth, eagerly awaits as the first boats row into the shallows.

"Now, my brave boys, are you ready?" he asks, heart in his throat.

"All ready," they reply.

"Fire!" the order is given.

Flash back. How has this swashbuckling captain/adventurer found himself at one of the pivotal moments in Hampton Roads—nay, American—history? Let's step back a couple of generations.

Emmerson's grandfather, the Reverend Arthur Emmerson, fetched up on these shores from Newcastle-on-Tyne, England. After marrying Ann Wishart from a prominent Princess Anne County family, they settled in the wilds of Assawoman Creek on the Eastern Shore and founded a church there. Their son, Arthur Emmerson II, started a school in Nansemond County, which, according to a newspaper ad, would teach "reading, writing and declamation," along with a smattering of languages. But he, too, was a man of the cloth and answered a call to a church in Suffolk, then Trinity Church in Portsmouth. The papers of his daughter, Louisa, describe him as a "bookish man with strong powers of concentration, and as a consequence, unobserving and absent-minded."

That wouldn't describe his son, Arthur Emmerson III. Born in 1778, he studied both for the ministry and the law but had a much stronger taste for life at sea. He signed on with merchant ships and was soon put in command of a Portsmouth schooner, *Rebecca*, which plied the sugar and rum routes to the West Indies. In 1798, as he was heading back to Hampton Roads, his vessel was taken as a prize by a French warship and he ended up as a prisoner in Marseilles. While on parole in that city, he learned the language so well that the Marquis de Lafayette, later visiting Portsmouth, would mistake him for a Frenchman.

Emmerson's career was cut short by nonimportation laws, so he bided his time in Portsmouth, trying his hand at business ventures. He married Mary Ann Herbert at her parents' home at Gosport. Their farm on the Southern Branch was to become part of the Gosport Navy Yard. The newlyweds set about the business of having twelve children—only four of whom lived to maturity.

In the meantime, he played soldier, forming a militia unit known as the Portsmouth Light Artillery Blues, and became its captain. It was this group of men whom he would lead into uncertain battle against foes who were determined to capture Norfolk, Portsmouth, the Navy Yard and perhaps the biggest prize, the frigate *Constellation*, then hemmed in on the Elizabeth River.

On the morning of June 22, they don't have long to wait. From the west, a party of seven hundred British soldiers and marines lands near Hoffler's Creek in Portsmouth—there's a wildlife refuge there now—and, after tromping through underbrush, attempts to wade across a narrow creek separating the mainland from Craney Island. The invaders are met by the withering fire of gunners, including several from the *Constellation*. Stumbling and disordered, they fall back across the creek and into nearby woods.

Now, Emmerson's gunners open up on the second attack from the barges, splintering some of the vessels and sending Royal Marines spilling into the water. It's over quickly, as the boats retreat to their ships. At least sixty, but perhaps two hundred, British troops lose their lives, while there's not a single American fatality. It's amazing how a far-inferior force held off the attack. It turned out to be one of the only land victories during the War of 1812.

Hampton Roads proudly celebrates what the state legislature deems the Battle of Craney Island Day in Virginia—a crucial moment in American history that the rest of the nation has largely ignored—even though the red glare of Congreve Rockets was seen here long before it was at Fort McHenry. And, fittingly, observers gather at the modest assembly of graves of the Emmerson family at historic Cedar Grove Cemetery in Portsmouth.

After the battle at Craney Island, Emmerson became an enduring local hero. He was a lifelong member of Trinity Church and served on the vestry for many years. He dabbled in politics, accepting the nod of the Whig

Craney Island, long a strategic gateway to Norfolk and Portsmouth, is shown as a "rebel battery," above, along with a similar battery at Sewell's Point. *Courtesy of the Mariners' Museum.*

Party to run for Congress, but was defeated by the Democratic nominee. He helped found the Portsmouth branch of the Bank of Virginia and, with other investors, the Portsmouth and Roanoke Railroad Co. It was one of the first in the nation, later becoming Seaboard Airline Railroad.

Emmerson was venerated throughout the rest of his life. A genealogical search found a request by the Light Artillery Blues for the pleasure of his company "at a social glass this afternoon at or near sunset. The company would also be glad to have any other Craney Island patriots who may be in the neighborhood to join them on this occasion."

Here's to you, Captain.

A DISMAL TALE

O ne of the joys of writing about history is finding little-known sources that take you directly to a time and place, old wine in brand-new bottles.

The story begins, as usual, with George Washington, surveyor, teaming up with a group of "adventurers" and buying forty thousand acres of the Great Dismal Swamp for the purpose of draining it, selling off its timber and developing it for farmland. Fortunately, the venture was a flop, although one of Washington's ideas, digging a canal to connect the waters of the Chesapeake Bay and the Albemarle Sound, had walking legs. It took years to get off the ground or, should we say, through the ground. Virginia in 1787 authorized digging the canal, but nothing happened until 1793, when work began.

The grueling, often brutal job of digging the twenty-two-mile Dismal Swamp Canal was carried out, naturally—who else would do this kind of work?—by slaves. One redeeming part of this miserable story is that some of the slaves, on loan from their owners and paid wages, were able to purchase freedom by the sweat of their brows. Another is that slaves, who had come to know the swamp better than anyone, often escaped there and hid out in its vast wilderness.

Now, like stumbling through a swamp into a clearing, I find this on the Internet: *Narrative of the Life of Moses Grandy, Late a Slave in the United States of America*, published in London in 1843. It is made available by the digitization project of the University of North Carolina, Chapel Hill. And here he is, talking about digging the canal!

> *The labour there is very severe. The ground is often very boggy: the negroes are up to the middle or much deeper in mud and water, cutting away roots and baling out mud: if they can keep their heads above water, they work on. They lodge in huts, or as they are called camps, made of shingles or boards.*

The Dismal Swamp Canal, built by slave labor and opened in 1805, is an alternative route on the Intracoastal Waterway. *Photo by Steve Earley, courtesy of* The Virginian-Pilot.

They lie down in the mud which has adhered to them, making a great fire to dry themselves, and keep off the cold. No bedding whatever is allowed them; it is only by work done over his task, that any of them can get a blanket. They are paid nothing except for this overwork. Their masters come once a month to receive the money for their labour: then perhaps some few very good masters will give them two dollars each, some others one dollar, some a pound of tobacco, and some nothing at all.

It wasn't until 1805 that a glorified ditch, with locks, opened for passage of poled, shallow-draft lighters carrying cedar shingles for houses. Much more digging was done and, at last, a wider, deeper canal opened. The first canalboat, bearing bacon and brandy from North Carolina, arrived at Norfolk in 1814.

The canal, now the oldest continuously operating canal in America and a linear member of the National Trust for Historic Preservation, is chronically threatened with closing as Congress stumbles through its budget swamp.

Like Moses Grandy, we seem unable to buy our freedom from this yearly story. Through backbreaking labor, working on barges that brought juniper shingles to market, he twice scraped together enough cash to buy his freedom, only to have his owners pocket the money and sell him. He endured. An admirer, Captain Edward Minner of Deep Creek, thought so much of Grandy that he purchased his freedom for $600, trusting him to pay it back. Grandy did, just managing to get away before he could be captured again. Then, working in sawmills and the Boston waterfront, he bought his wife and son out of slavery.

What I'll remember most about this guy is his jubilation on finally obtaining his freedom: "I felt myself so light, that I almost thought I could fly, and in my sleep I was always dreaming of flying over woods and rivers."

The woods and rivers in our backyard.

A MESMERIC FIGURE

If you were to wander through a small residential neighborhood behind Norfolk's Riverside Corporate Center, you'd find a couple of luxury home developments sprouting beside the eastern branch of the Elizabeth River. At water's edge, piers and boat slips are being built. Off to the left, traffic hums across the Military Highway Bridge.

There's no marker, road name or any other indication that the land here was probably once called "Rolleston" and that it was bought in 1860 by the man who, almost single-handedly, propelled Virginia into the Confederacy and the Civil War.

Henry A. Wise, born in Accomack County, had bought an 884-acre plantation in Princess Anne County in 1960 after serving as a member of Congress and then governor. He became something of a local hero because of his role in sending radical abolitionist John Brown to the gallows in October 1859. There was talk of a presidential bid, but Wise's claim to fame then was to rally support for "committees of safety" that would raise arms against the government in the event that Abe Lincoln was elected president. These "Princess Anne Resolves" weren't taken very seriously, but Wise's real impact on history was about to be felt.

There's a book by Richmond historian Nelson D. Lankford, *Cry Havoc!*, that focuses on Virginia's role—with great emphasis on the architect of the state's slide toward war. He paints Wise as a hothead who probably did more to prod the state, and with it the rest of the reluctant upper South, into the conflict.

At first, a solid majority at a special convention held near the capitol in January 1861 opposed secession. Not even Wise, try as he might, could sway many votes. "Though he appeared much older than his fifty-four years, he was a figure of mesmeric intensity," Lankford writes. "Erratic, slovenly,

The plantation owned by Henry A. Wise, who spearheaded Virginia's secession from the Union, was taken over by the government after the Civil War to teach former slaves to read and write. *Courtesy of the Sargeant Memorial Room of the Norfolk Public Library.*

gesticulating as he spoke, dribbling tobacco juice down the front of his linen shirt, contorting his face and waving his hands, Wise in full cry was unmistakable."

After months of numbing deliberation and delays, the first vote on secession was held on April 4, and it went down to defeat: forty-five to ninety, with prominent Hampton Roads delegates siding with the unionist majority. Leaders of upper South states like North Carolina, Arkansas and Maryland breathed sighs of relief that the prestigious Old Dominion had so resoundingly stood its ground.

But two events quickly tilted the stage in the other direction. First, on April 12, Confederate batteries at Charleston Harbor opened fire on Fort Sumter, forcing the evacuation of Federal forces there. The attack was deliberately designed to provoke Lincoln, and it worked. Two days later, the president issued a call for seventy-five thousand soldiers to put down the rebellion, with the still-loyal upper Southern states taking part. Virginia's quota was to be four regiments.

The once-solid pro-Union sentiment throughout the upper South quickly crumbled as leaders railed against sending troops to subdue neighboring states. The secession convention reassembled and Henry Wise, "gaunt, intense and mercurial," in Lankford's description, craved vindication. Still, several prominent Virginians, including some who would later reluctantly don gray uniforms, opposed him. But as he rose to speak, Wise pulled out a large pistol and waved it in a menacing flourish. There was no time for more debate, he declared, revealing that he had taken matters into his own hands and engineered an attack on the Federal arsenal at Harper's Ferry. He and others had met in his hotel room and agreed to send telegrams to militias in the Shenandoah Valley to proceed with the attack. The convention stampeded, voting eighty-eight to fifty-five to secede.

North Carolina, Arkansas and Tennessee quickly joined the Confederacy, although Maryland narrowly declined, and the western part of Virginia split off to form a new state. A brutal war followed, with the loss of 600,000 men and a devastating blow to an entire region. Wise served as brigadier general in the Confederate army and survived the war he helped ignite. When he returned to Tidewater, he was shocked by what he found.

His estate and mansion had been taken over by the Federal government and former slaves were being taught there by missionaries to read and write. He eventually regained title to Rolleston but never returned to live there, and not long after, the mansion was destroyed by fire. An 1866 map in Stephen S. Mansfield's book about Princess Anne County shows the location of the Wise tract. It was subsequently annexed by Norfolk.

A cool breeze greeted a visitor who stood on a pier jutting out into the river. Crows in nearby pine trees chattered raucously. Neither on the subdivided lots facing the river, nor among the rubble piled on the beach, was there any sign that a powerful and defiant figure had once walked here.

FALLEN WARRIORS

O n a cloudy March morning, a cool breeze off the York River mingles with the scent of onion grass that sprouts among flat headstones at Yorktown National Cemetery. John Hort, a retired army lieutenant colonel, moves from grave site to grave site, smoothing the ground around the rectangular markers, cutting back weeds and dusting the stones with a broom.

"I guess these are my fallen warriors," says Hort, a seventy-one-year-old Vietnam veteran who has been tending these graves as a volunteer for more than twenty years. "Hopefully some day somebody will do this for me."

This small cemetery rests on hallowed ground, right next to the American and French siege lines that sealed the fate of the British army on another cool dawn, in October 1781. But these fallen soldiers were from the Civil War, and the first of these perished in the stubborn, bloody battles of the Peninsula Campaign 145 years ago.

One week after the March 9 battle of the ironclads, a massive army of more than 120,000 men began sailing down the Chesapeake Bay and landing at Fort Monroe. Under the meticulous but famously foot-dragging General George B. McClellan, the Union forces engaged in several punishing battles and then decided on a massive siege. By the time McClellan had readied all the troops, horses and heavy artillery, it amounted to the largest strike force ever assembled in America.

Rebel units had occupied Yorktown, building breastworks on top of the old British ones. Vastly outnumbered and outgunned, they knew they could hold out for no more than a few hours. And they also knew exactly when the attack would come. On the night of May 3, the Rebels staged an artillery barrage to mask their movements, all the while stealing away. In the morning, when the great siege was to begin, the enemy had vanished.

Union troops set up camp at Yorktown where Confederate fortifications had been erected. A national cemetery is located there, near one-time British defenses. *Courtesy of the National Archives.*

A frustrated Union soldier wrote home, "The southern buzzard has flown the roost!" according to Adrian Wheat, a retired army surgeon who has made this part of history his specialty.

The Yankees charged off in hot pursuit and there were battles all up and down the peninsula, but the Southern forces succeeded in bogging down McClellan's mighty army at Williamsburg and in the swamps near the Chickahominy River, finally driving him off in disgrace. The great peninsula strategy of capturing Richmond and putting a quick end to the war was a miserable failure.

Here on this forlorn spot overlooking the river are many who paid the price. Diane DePew, a National Park Service historian who accompanies me, can tell by dates on the markers where the different soldiers fell. For instance, those bearing the date April 16—like Private Ezekiel Waterman of the Third Vermont Infantry—were likely killed at Dam No. 1 south of Yorktown. Forty-four Vermont soldiers were killed there. One who died on April 17 likely lingered until the next day.

On the other hand, those whose deaths don't correspond to a battle were surely the victims of disease that spread throughout the camps. For every two killed in action, five died from disease, DePew says. Many were never identified. Sadly, more than half of the approximately two thousand soldiers here are unknown, many lying two and three—and in one case, four—to a grave. Some were sharpshooters cut down by their counterparts on the other side.

And then there's this: scattered among the flat, rectangular markers are those of both "colored" and Confederate units, young men from vastly different backgrounds who, after the rage and sorrow of war is over, now lie close to one another on this lonely ground.

And now a retired lieutenant colonel who served in a much different kind of war tends their graves and sets out flags on them each Memorial Day.

FREEDOM'S FORTRESS

If you're wondering why historians and others are so passionate about Fort Monroe and its future after the army leaves in 2011, consider this: on the night of May 23, 1861, three slaves belonging to Charles Mallory, a powerful lawyer and Confederate officer in Hampton, summoned the courage to escape. They slipped away from a work party at Sewell's Point, jumped in a skiff and rowed across Hampton Roads to the fort, where they asked for protection.

Their timing couldn't have been better. The escapees, Sheppard Mallory, Frank Baker and James Townsend, went before the fort's new commanding officer, Major General Benjamin F. Butler, who seemed to have a habit of stirring up controversy. He quizzed them sharply. Then, when Confederate major John Cary came to the fort under a flag of truce and demanded that the runaways be returned under the Fugitive Slave Act, Butler refused, calling them "contrabands of war."

Word of their fate spread rapidly. On Cornell University's "Making of America" website, I found this account by a Union private, published in *Harper's Weekly*:

> *On Sunday morning, May 26, eight negroes stood before the quarters of General Butler, waiting for an audience...On May 27th, forty-seven negroes of both sexes and all ages, from three months to eighty-five years, among whom were half a dozen entire families, came in one squad. Another lot of a dozen good field-hands arrived the same day; and then they continued to come by twenties, thirties, and forties.*

By June 10, the soldier said, as his unit was preparing for battle at a place called Big Bethel, a group of runaways "inquired anxiously the way to 'the freedom fort.'"

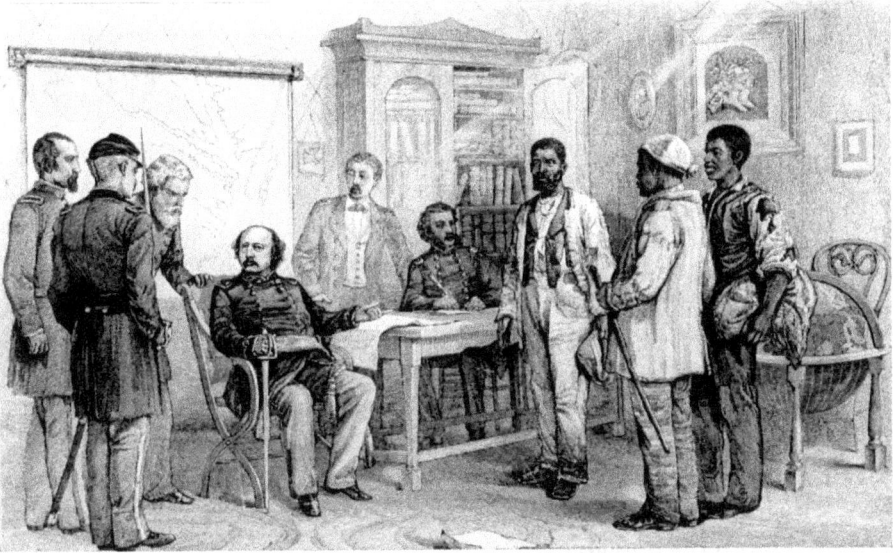

General Benjamin F. Butler declared escaped slaves "contraband" of war, setting the stage for emancipation. *Courtesy of the Hampton History Museum.*

The trickle of runaway slaves turned into a flood and then a torrent. When all was said and done, at least ten thousand former slaves had taken refuge behind Union lines near Hampton. Furthermore, the scenario was repeated throughout the South as former slaves declared themselves to be "contrabands."

The official record of Union and Confederate navies during the war has the following entry for August 6, 1861. With respect to vessels "found conveying negroes for the purpose of aiding or comforting the rebellion, such negroes, if they desire, will be permitted to come to Fortress Monroe where they will be employed and cared for. B.F. Butler, major general, commanding." So this simple act of self-dignity had directly influenced official policy of the United States Army.

It was not emancipation, not yet. Professor Robert F. Engs, in his book *Freedom's First Generation*, points out that President Lincoln was hoping that the insurrection would soon be over and didn't want to stir things up. But refusing to return contrabands of war was acceptable. Lincoln let Butler's decision stand. Congress passed the Confiscation Acts of 1862, providing for the freedom of slaves escaping from Southern owners. Lincoln issued his proclamation in September.

The point is not that a handful of slaves were given their freedom by a suddenly enlightened white general or by presidential proclamation, but that they had the audacity, in the face of overwhelming odds and decades of onerous federal laws condoning slavery, to assert their rights as human beings.

Consultants for the city of Hampton have presented various options, all of which preserve most of the fort's historic areas but allow private residential development. Citizens for Fort Monroe National Park contends that the entire 570 acres, not just the moated stone fortress, should be parkland.

Following the example of San Francisco's Presidio, a former military base that now leases historic buildings for commercial use, park proponents say the much more historic Fort Monroe deserves national park status. If recognized for what it is, the place where slavery began to crumble, they say, tourists from around the world would make it a must-see destination.

"Freedom's Fortress" could become a national symbol for a great moment in American history, where a candle was lit in the cathedral of the human spirit that has refused to go out.

My Gift to You

Gerri Hollins has part of Hampton's history flowing through her veins. She's a descendant of the "contrabands," the thousands of slaves who fled from their masters during the Civil War and took refuge behind Union lines. She's devoting this part of her life to telling—and singing—their story.

"It is a story of the beginning of the end of slavery in the United States," she said recently at her home on West Queen Street. She wore an African "royal robe" from Togo and cradled a cane from Ghana that she called a "griot," one that belongs to a storyteller. Her dog Cyrus panted softly as a floor fan whirred.

A teacher and singer-songwriter, Hollins may have a lot to do with whether the story of the contrabands' struggle for freedom is told in a way that helps preserve the legacy of Fort Monroe. The army will leave the fort in 2011, but the stage is being set right now as to how its future plays out.

It was in "Fortress Monroe," as it was called then, that in April 1861 three escaped slaves appealed for protection and were judged to be "contrabands of war." Some ten thousand slaves soon took refuge behind Union lines and thousands more in other parts of the South, creating the momentum, historians say, that led to emancipation. That movement also put an indelible stamp on Hampton.

When Union troops by the thousands descended upon the peninsula shortly after Virginia joined the Confederacy, almost the entire white population of Hampton packed up and fled. As they did so, Southern forces burned the city to the ground, but almost before the smoke cleared, the people whom Robert Engs has called "Freedom's First Generation" moved back in and reclaimed it.

Gerri Hollins of Hampton is a descendant of the "contrabands," the former slaves granted their freedom after fleeing to Fort Monroe. *Photo by Steve Earley, courtesy of* The Virginian-Pilot.

Hollins said,

> *They resurrected the downtown area from the ashes. They named Lincoln Street, Union Street, Grant Street and Liberty Street, now Armistead Avenue. They made a moral, spiritual, economically viable community for former slaves. And when the Southerners came back and moved outside downtown, the slaves reached out to help them get back on their feet. They didn't have any malice in their hearts. They just wanted to be free, and to live and raise their families and not be torn apart.*

Among these new urban pioneers were Hollins's great-great-grandparents, one of whom had been sold to a family in Hampton.

Hollins, who grew up in Hampton, went to the University of Michigan and then to New York in hopes of becoming an opera singer, but she spent most of her singing career as a backup singer while teaching at Harlem School for the Arts. In 1991, after twenty-five years, she decided it was time to come home and "give back."

Besides serving as president of the Contraband Historical Society and a member of the board of Citizens for Fort Monroe National Park, she has written and directed a video, *Freedom's Fortress, the Contraband Slave Story*, and a folk opera, *Prelude to Freedom, The Contraband Slave Story*, performed in 2005 at Thomas Nelson Community College. And, as she says, with a little help from the Lord, she conceived and designed the Contraband Living History Museum for Southern Culture. It may seem ambitious, she realizes, but she feels that the contraband movement deserves no less.

> *146 years later, there's nothing here in the city of Hampton, there's nothing at Fort Monroe that speaks to this, nothing. These are special people, they come from all walks of life, and we're working together to make sure that there's a legacy for the young people, you know, so they can follow an example of real heroes and sheroes back in the days, who made sense of it all. Despite their human suffering, they were able to overcome enormous obstacles, to become revered by their ancestors. Had it not been for those people, where would we be?*

Before I left, Hollins sang for me. Moving to her piano, she sang in a rich alto voice the song that ends her folk opera. The character is Mary Peake, the former Hampton slave who risked her life to teach children to read and write.

> *I will love in the morning light,*
> *I'll protect you in the dark of night,*
> *You will know that I'll be there*
> *To guide you through the day,*
> *I will love you even when I'm gone,*
> *And my love will help you carry on,*
> *How I will love you,*
> *My gift to you.*
> *My gift to you.*
> *My gift to you.*

GRANITE BASTION

O kay, history lovers, here's today's quiz. What place in Hampton Roads did President Andrew Jackson consider his summer retreat? Or another president, John Tyler, his retreat from sorrow? On what spot did Abraham Lincoln stand to watch the Union attack on Norfolk? Or for that matter, where did a new long-range gun sit while lobbing shells at Sewell's Point? Furthermore, where can you stand today and capture a panoramic view of the Hampton Roads waterway and the cities that surround it?

Clue: it's connected to the man-made island where northbound cars duck into the tunnel part of the Hampton Roads Bridge Tunnel (HRBT). It's... Fort Wool, one of the most historic and scenic places in Hampton Roads and yet one of the least known.

It's no wonder. You can't stop while driving through the HRBT—and if you try to catch a glimpse while approaching the tunnel you could get yourself killed. The only safe way to see the fort is to take one of the harbor tours that leave from downtown Hampton. The boat, *Miss Hampton II*, calls briefly at the island.

Much to my luck, Hampton History Museum curator Michael Cobb is writing a book on the fort and offers to take me out there. The fort belongs to the state but is under the care of the city. And he, being the fort buff that he is—you might say forts are his forte—loves being there.

After scrambling over the granite jetty that connects the island with the tunnel, we stand near one of the decommissioned gun turrets facing the harbor. It's an amazing vantage point, surrounded by the water that caresses the shorelines of most of the region's cities. The history of the place seems to flow along with it. "When you're here you really do have a sense of the past, a sense of the people who were here before," Cobb says.

Fort Wool, sitting on a man-made island across from Fort Monroe in Hampton Roads, created a near-impregnable gauntlet for hostile ships. *Courtesy of the Hampton History Museum.*

After the British sailed unmolested into regional waters during the War of 1812, burning Washington and sacking Hampton, the country decided on a series of coastal defenses. Part of that strategy was to build Fort Monroe, and then, in order to subject invaders to a murderous crossfire, a companion fort on a shoal just off Willoughby Spit.

Work began in 1819. It was a monster job, creating an artificial island with tons of granite blocks. They were hauled down from a quarry near Washington, D.C., and dumped onto the shoal, until gradually the fifteen-acre island appeared. The cornerstone of the new fort was laid in September 1826, but the heavier the massive fortress became the more it settled and the more granite had to be added. One of the army engineers who supervised was a young second lieutenant, Robert E. Lee.

The fort was named for John C. Calhoun, a South Carolinian who became secretary of war during the Monroe administration. But it was commonly called "the Rip Raps" after the rocky shoal on which it stood. During the Civil War, the southerner's name was stripped away and the honor was bestowed on General John E. Wool, the commander of Fort Monroe.

It was during the war that the experimental, rifled Sawyer gun was tried out, bombarding Confederate batteries at Sewell's Point. And during May 1862, Lincoln watched a botched attempt to capture Sewell's Point and then the successful landing at Ocean View.

But the moments for which the fort is best known were not about war. President Jackson paid a visit in July 1829 and "took a minute view of that stupendous fortification," according to a paper on the fort by Chester D. Bradley. There was something wondrous about the place to the Tennessean, who came back for eleven days in August, "inhaling the salubrious ocean breezes and daily taking the salt water bath." He returned for several other summer vacations.

In the fall of 1842, President Tyler, mourning the death of his wife, went into seclusion at the fort, staying at the same residence that Jackson had enjoyed. This modest "hotel" was leveled by fire a few years later.

Fort Wool fell into disuse after the Civil War but enjoyed a rebirth at the turn of the century during the Spanish-American War and then again during World Wars I and II. Each time, new fortifications were erected and gun mounts installed. The guns were fired in practice but never again in anger.

As Cobb and I stroll along the ramparts, container ships and a navy frigate crisscross out in the channel, and off to the east, a pod of dolphins splashes. We can smell the salt air and hear waves lapping on the granite foundations.

"For me," he says, "the sound and the smell of the water is timeless, and it was experienced for the first time by people who set foot on this island."

A MOST UNUSUAL
PRESIDENTIAL VISIT

Abe Lincoln attacks Norfolk!

That might have been the headline in the *Norfolk Daily News*, had there had been such a publication, on May 10, 1862, when the Republican president personally supervised the landing that secured Union control of the city.

In an extraordinary act by a commander in chief, Lincoln studied military strategy at the Library of Congress, then jumped on a boat that took him down the Potomac to the Chesapeake Bay and then to Fort Monroe. He stopped briefly to tour the Union ironclad *Monitor* and then decided on the attack at Ocean View.

Recently, old Abe himself—or at least a reasonable facsimile, nationally known Lincoln interpreter George Buss—held a press conference at Fort Norfolk to give his views on the capture. His visit was sponsored by the Norfolk Historical Society and Citizens for Fort Monroe National Park. At the same time, a Civil War encampment took place at the fort.

Buss, from Freeport, Illinois, where the second Lincoln-Douglas debate took place, portrayed Lincoln at the opening of the Monitor Center in March. The tall and lanky schoolteacher, with chin-strap beard and stovepipe hat, looks and acts the role pretty convincingly.

"As Paul Simon says, 'It's every American's duty to get right with Lincoln,'" Buss tells me.

Lincoln was exasperated by the lack of progress by General George McClellan, who was supposed to have sent his huge invading force on the road to Richmond but was repeatedly stalled. "He had placed so many hopes and dreams on what McClellan had told him he could accomplish," Buss said.

So Lincoln did what he figured he had to do—take command.

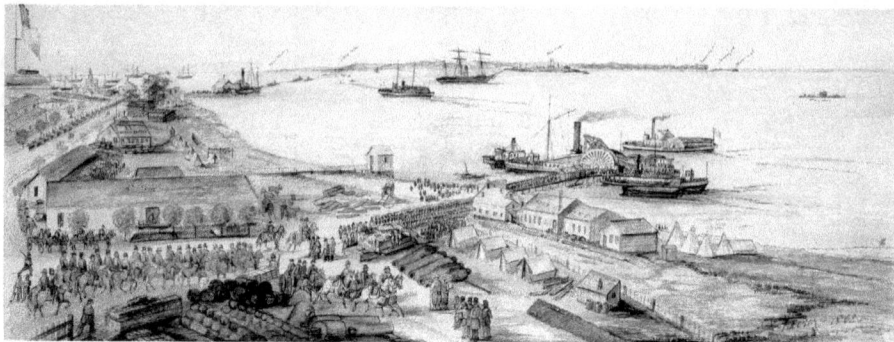

Union troops boarding waiting vessels near Fort Monroe for an invasion of Norfolk. Lincoln is depicted in the middle foreground in a stovepipe hat. *Courtesy of the Mariners' Museum.*

The story goes that he and Secretary of the Treasury Salmon P. Chase were rowed across Hampton Roads to Ocean View in a longboat. By then the Confederate forces were in retreat, and when the lone sentry still on duty fled as they approached, Lincoln said this was where they should land.

It was evening, May 9, when a force of six thousand Union troops under General John Wool, then commander at Fort Monroe, boarded all manner of watercraft near the fort and sailed across to Ocean View. The next morning, after a circuitous march because of burning bridges, the troops were met at Princess Anne Road and Church Street by Mayor William Lamb and members of city council carrying a flag of truce.

"I'm not aware of any other time in American history where a president has taken an active role in directing troops in war," said Louis Guy, president of the Norfolk Historical Society. Guy's great-grandfather, Elias Guy, was "captain of the watch," the equivalent of police chief, at the time, and he believes it was the latter's house, with white flag flying, that was pictured in a *Harper's Weekly* sketch of the confrontation.

After a brief conference, Wool and his party accompanied Lamb downtown, either to the steps of city hall or the customshouse. There Lamb read what must have been one of the longest surrender proclamations in history while, across the Elizabeth, Confederate forces put the Gosport Navy Yard to the torch before fleeing.

In the meantime, Southern commanders realized that the *Virginia*, the South's ironclad marauder, had no place to go except the bottom of the Elizabeth River. The ship was run aground at Craney Island and blown up. In a matter of days, all of Hampton Roads, from Virginia Beach to Suffolk, Hampton to Newport News, was in Union hands. The secession here had lasted from April 20, 1861, to May 10, 1862.

Lincoln never set foot in Norfolk. But, anxious to find out how the attack went, he sailed up the Elizabeth River to Norfolk Harbor to see for himself before departing for Washington.

The fall of Norfolk may have ended the war locally, but it wasn't the end for many local sons who fought and died elsewhere as the brutal war continued. One Norfolk County schoolgirl, Katie Darling Wallace, age eleven, lamented in a letter to the editor of a local paper in January 1864, "All our dear boys...are gone to war. May they be spared to the end of this dreadful carnage."

CLASH OF IRON

On the night of March 8, 1862, while the CSS *Virginia* lay at anchor at Sewell's Point, a pilot onboard thought he saw a strange shape glide by out on Hampton Roads. It was a silhouette, really, the shape of a water tank on a raft, backlit by the fires of a burning Federal ship. What an incredible scene that must have been.

The crew members of the *Virginia* were celebrating. That day they had dealt a devastating blow to the Union, mauling two powerful Union warships and sending shockwaves all the way to Washington. The rest of the Federal blockade ships awaited them in the morning. It would be a walk in the park.

Meanwhile, the surreptitious vessel dropped anchor out on the Roads.

The amazing thing to me about the battle of Hampton Roads is not so much the clash of the ironclads and the dawn of a new era in naval warfare but the fact that the two threads of history were so improbably spun together.

Here was the USS *Merrimack*, caught at the Gosport Navy Yard when war broke out, risen from the dead and cloaked in iron that was melted down from trolley tracks. Here were artillery gunners mustered off the forts at Norfolk and sent into battle without so much as a sea trial. And here was this unlikely Yankee opponent, riveted together on a Brooklyn waterfront in just over three months and now entering the field of combat that we can see from our modern bridge tunnels. The USS *Monitor*, too, was sent to sea in a most untried and unseaworthy condition—and almost didn't make it to Hampton Roads.

It was a nightmarish trip down the Atlantic, with water pouring through every conceivable opening in torrents, filling the engine room with smoke as water reached the fires. Apparently lifeless firemen had to be carried to the top of the turret and revived with fresh air and brandy. After two days and two sleepless nights, the ship rounded Cape Charles on the afternoon of March 8. In the distance the crew heard heavy gunfire.

The Union ship *Monitor*, with its revolutionary swiveling turret, blasts away at its Confederate counterpart in Hampton Roads. *Lithograph by J.O. Davidson, courtesy of the Mariners' Museum.*

As they entered Hampton Roads that night, they could see the masts of the USS *Cumberland* jutting from the water like fence posts, and just as they got ready to anchor, the *Congress* went up in a fearsome explosion. "It went straight to the marrow of our bones," said Dana Greene, the *Monitor's* executive officer.

Fog lay on the roads the next morning but soon burned off as the sun rose. And just as it did, the watch on the Union ship noticed the *Virginia* steaming away from Sewell's Point. As the Rebel ship approached, the North's champion slid from out of the shadow of the USS *Minnesota*, the next likely victim. Ignoring whatever impertinence lay before them, the *Virginia's* gunners opened up on the *Minnesota*. William Keeler, the *Monitor's* paymaster, stumbled below and took stock of his chances of survival. "We were enclosed in what we supposed to be impenetrable armor—we knew that a powerful foe was about to meet us—ours was an untried experiment and our enemy's first fire might make it a coffin for us all."

Then the Confederates saw something strange happen. The great turret on the vessel in their path slowly swiveled toward them, a port swung open and a huge cannon—eleven inches wide—was run out and fired. The second battle of Hampton Roads had been joined.

They battled for four hours, circling like punch-drunk fighters, actually touching a couple of times. The gunners on both ships stripped down to their waists, grunting in their hellish confines as they loaded, rammed and fired, wincing as monstrous shots clanged against their armor, collapsing as the four-hour contest ended in a draw.

For us in this region, as well as maybe hundreds of thousands of others from around the country, the lucky part is that this titanic clash has been recreated in all its intensity for the Battle Theater of the new Monitor Center in Newport News. It opened on March 9, 2007, 145 years after this intriguing intersection of warfare and technology.

INTO THE ABYSS

This is about logs. Not the kind you toss on the fire but the kind you keep while standing watch on a ship at sea, carefully observing and recording everything you can about that intimate universe of sea and sky around you. Time, boat speed and heading, wind speed and direction, current position, barometer, sea state, weather conditions and a lot more. These observations, made at regular intervals, tell a story about a ship's passage and its life on the water. And, at critical moments, the events that make history.

It was thrilling to see, in the library of the Mariners' Museum, a copy of the first log of the ironclad ship *Monitor*, lying open in a large bound book that was cradled on a reading table there. The first entry is matter-of-fact, but I couldn't help wondering what Lieutenant John Worden, the new commander, must have felt when he awoke onboard the ship in the Brooklyn Navy Yard and wrote: "February 27 comes in cloudy weather, light wind from N.E. 2 a.m. Commenced snowing."

Or the moment, just over a week later, when the *Monitor* rounded Cape Charles after a terrifying night on the open sea and the watch officer noted the sound of heavy gunfire in the direction of Hampton Roads. Again, you can't tell what he thought, but that single observation must have been accompanied by all kinds of emotions, not the least of them dread.

But the most fascinating document is the one that the National Archives sent me: a copy of the log of the side-wheel steamer *Rhode Island*, made on December 30, 1862.

The *Rhode Island* was the towship that accompanied the *Monitor* on its last journey as it left Hampton Roads and headed south. Because the ironclad's log did not survive, its escort's record of the passage is loaded with significance. And if you didn't know anything else about the fate of the ship,

The wreck of the *Monitor*, from a wooden engraving in *Harper's Weekly*, January 24, 1863. *Courtesy of the Mariners' Museum.*

this document says it all. The story just about jumps off the page when you realize what is going on.

The first thing you notice, beginning at 1:00 a.m., is the wind speed, which in those days was denoted as Force 0-12 on the Beaufort scale, ranging from dead calm at 0 to howling hurricane at 12. The entry says "1," meaning almost no wind, at most three knots, from the south-southwest. If the officer on watch could have seen the water at that point, he might have noticed a pattern of scaly ripples on the surface.

Both the water and air temperatures are fifty degrees at this point, pretty warm for a winter night on the Atlantic, and there is a barometer reading of 30.12. I guess you'd call it a Bermuda high. The ships move at a brisk clip of seven knots, with depth readings of eighteen to twenty fathoms.

The night passes uneventfully, with no change in wind speed. The barometer holds steady as a runner's heartbeat and the air and sea temperatures begin to rise as they encounter the Gulf Stream. Soon after, during the noon-to-four watch, there's this entry: "At 1 p.m., made Cape Hatteras Light House bearing W.S.W. distance 14 miles. Sounded in 17 fathoms." You can almost hear the snoozing.

But anyone who has experienced warm winter days around here knows that sooner or later things are going to change. And usually unpleasantly.

It begins gradually that evening. At 7:00 p.m., as the crew members are finishing their evening meal, the wind speed jumps from Force 1 to 3 (ten knots or so) and there's a subtle dip in the barometer, now reading 30.00. A low-pressure system, dragging cold air down out of the north, is approaching. The cloud bank that some of the crewmen noticed in the morning is the leading edge of the front and it's about to crash the party, exchanging energy with the warm, moist air over the ocean.

By 8:00 p.m., the wind has freshened to Force 4, up to sixteen knots. At about 9:00 p.m., the front arrives and the wind starts to moan. The entry says Force 6, meaning winds of twenty-two to twenty-seven knots and white-capped waves up to thirteen feet. The barometer continues its plunge.

And then here's this chilling entry in the log: "At 11 she made signal of distress. Stopped, hailed her and was informed she was in a sinking condition."

We know the rest of the story. More than one thousand artifacts from the sunken ship, including the 120-ton turret, an engine, two big guns and a ring found on the hand of a skeleton, are on display or undergoing conservation at the Mariners' Museum. We can see for ourselves the end of the tale that the logs began.

FOLLY IT WAS NOT

The house has many stories. Of love, hatred, war and sadness. But, first of all, ridicule.

So grandiose was the Greek Revival mansion Mills Riddick built on North Main Street in Suffolk that busybodies thought he was more than a bit touched. Twenty-one rooms, sixteen fireplaces! Heart pine floors and faux stone walls! No good could come of such extravagance. Riddick's Folly, that's what they'd call it.

Riddick, a prominent businessman and politician, may have had the last laugh. He and his wife, Mary Taylor Riddick, had fourteen children, ten of whom survived infancy. Their well-populated home surely was one of the social centers of town. But Riddick lived only seven years after the house was completed in 1837, and his children, who inherited a world rapidly turning upside down, could be said to have had the first honest-to-goodness cry.

If you're wondering why Riddick's Folly is peopled annually by Union and Confederate reenactors, as well as those from the United Daughters of the Confederacy—as part of History and Heritage Weekend—consider the folly that befell the Riddicks. After Mills Riddick's death in 1844, his son Nathaniel, a judge, took over the place and ran it until the war overwhelmed the town. It was May 1862, and Norfolk had just surrendered to Union forces. In Suffolk, the scramble to get out of town must have been chaotic. Most of the well-to-do families, including the Riddicks, packed up whatever they could carry, burying silver and china in the backyard, and then boarded trains and fled. Two days later, mounted soldiers from New York rode into town, the first of thousands who would follow.

The eldest daughter of Nathaniel and Missouri Riddick, Anna Mary, undoubtedly took it the hardest. Her story—from the dark, brooding painting of a storm-battered seacoast in the foyer to the silk dresses and ring

Riddick's Folly, so named because of its size, at the time of the Civil War; it is now a museum in Suffolk. *Courtesy of Riddick's Folly.*

on the third floor, to the blood-soaked floorboards on the fourth—echoes throughout the mansion.

The gold ring, woven with dark human hair, was given to Anna Mary by a tutor, Jonathan Smith, on the day he left to fight in the war. If they were engaged, no one knew, but it was clear that "Jonny" had a place in her heart. He wrote her affectionate, almost daily letters from the front until July 1862, when he was cut down, along with thousands of others, attempting to storm Union positions at Malvern Hill near Richmond. Anna Mary, who lived to be ninety-five, never married, but it was clear that she kept his memory alive. Along with her hatred of the North.

One good reason was that the Union troops, under the command of Major General John Peck, used the house as their headquarters. It was strategically situated, with clear views—especially from fourth-story windows—of the Nansemond River, the town and the distant countryside. When they left near the end of the war, they ransacked the place and took most of the furnishings. They left behind graffiti and blood.

A fourth-floor children's room has got to be one of the most fascinating parts of any house museum in America. "Yanks, you ought to be here," one of the scrawled and puzzling messages says. "Know we would give a good time. Go home and stay there."

And then there's the large bloodstain in the floor. Phillip Staten, the new director of Riddick's Folly, told me on a tour that the best guess why the room was never restored was that Anna Mary kept her letters from Jonny and her memories of the war under lock and key there.

If you think Riddick's Folly was mere folly, look again.

IMMENSE DIGNITY

It's no bigger than a postcard or page from an artist's sketchpad, but with all the details and intimacy of a photograph captured in a split second of time. This remarkable watercolor portrait of a young slave girl by the woman who was soon to become the wife of Robert E. Lee was recently acquired by the Colonial Williamsburg Foundation and is now on display at the DeWitt-Wallace Museum.

The portrait by Mary Anna Randolph Custis shows a young girl carrying a water tub, with a minimal background of fencing and hills that makes her stand out. She's looking straight at the artist. Although clearly attentive, there's a quiet self-assurance that you would not see in one-dimensional, stereotypical drawings of slaves that were typical of the period, says Barbara Luck, curator of paintings, drawings and sculpture at the foundation. "I think you sense this is a real child who may have stood there just like this," Luck says, standing before the portrait.

It is likely that Custis knew the girl, perhaps from childhood at Arlington House, the 1,100-acre plantation on the Potomac that would become Arlington National Cemetery. She would have grown up among many of the nearly two hundred slaves owned by her father, George Washington Parke Custis, the adopted grandson of George Washington.

Mary Custis held a lifelong concern for the education of slaves. Her mother believed in teaching them to read and write in preparation for eventual emancipation.

The portrait is dated 1830. The next year, Custis married Lee, her childhood playmate and distant cousin. Lee spent the next thirty years in the U.S. Army, serving, among other duties, as superintendent at the U.S. Military Academy at West Point, New York. Lee apparently had the small portrait with him. He gave it to one of his most promising

A postcard-size watercolor of a slave girl, by Mary Anna Randolph Custis, who was to marry Robert E. Lee. *Courtesy of the Colonial Williamsburg Foundation.*

cadets, J.E.B. Stuart. (The museum obtained it at an auction of Stuart memorabilia.)

Lee's father-in-law had stipulated in his will that his slaves be freed upon his death—provided that Arlington House was in good financial condition— but no later than five years afterward. He must have known that the finances were in trouble. When his father-in-law died in 1857, Lee had to take a leave from the army and return home to straighten up the mess. He determined that the only way to do it was with slave labor.

According to historian Elizabeth Brown Pryor, who has just written a book about Lee based on previously unknown letters, he was a hard taskmaster. Some of his slaves were hired out to friends and sent elsewhere, breaking up families that had been together on the estate for generations. Many resented him, and he was forced to put down a revolt by severely whipping some of the men.

Because of his late father-in-law's wishes, Lee finally freed the slaves. Coincidentally, they gained their freedom on January 1, 1863, the date President Lincoln's Emancipation Proclamation went into effect.

Lee has long been considered antislavery because of the letter he wrote to Mary in 1856. "In this enlightened age," he wrote, "there are few I believe, but what will acknowledge, that slavery as an institution, is a moral and political evil in any Country."

That would have cemented his legacy as a renegade among peers. But then, as though others might be looking over his shoulder, he goes on to mimic the prevailing sentiment that slaves are "immeasurable better off here than in Africa, morally, socially & physically. The painful discipline they are undergoing, is necessary for their instruction as a race, & I hope will prepare & lead them to better things. How long their subjugation may be necessary is known & ordered by a wise Merciful Providence."

You have to wonder what Mary, who saw the immense dignity in those young eyes, must have thought.

SKETCHES OF WAR

On nice days, she sometimes walks the beach near Fort Story and ponders an improbable scene: a Union vessel, paddle wheels churning the water close to shore, Confederate militia suddenly appearing from the woods. An exchange of gunfire. Curses, shaken fists. A young sailor onboard writing and sketching in a notebook, his heart in his throat.

"Gosh, to think it happened right here," says Barbara Ferguson of Virginia Beach. "How could he imagine he'd have a granddaughter who some day would be standing there and looking at that spot?"

And how could John Fentress, a cavalry captain who patrolled the shoreline and fired on the Union vessel, have imagined that his great-great-grandson would serve in the government of a place called Virginia Beach? And that his distant relative would one day work with the descendant of one of those Yankees on plans for the city's future?

What alerted Ferguson to this remarkable coincidence begins with the Civil War letters, maps, logbooks and sketches of her grandfather, Thomas Farrell, discovered in brown paper bags in a Philadelphia home after her uncle passed away. They include dozens of pages of descriptions of Farrell's war experiences and meticulous drawings of enemy positions that made him one of the most useful observers during the war—and at one point a Union spy.

Farrell, who came to this country from Ireland at the age of three, was an eighteen-year-old third mate aboard the side-wheel steamer *Quaker City*, which had been privately commissioned to chase down Confederate blockade runners trying to make for the open sea near Hampton Roads. During five months in these waters, *Quaker City* captured or helped capture ten vessels attempting to skirt the Union blockade.

In the meantime, the Northern privateer, stationed at Lynnhaven Bay, made life interesting for local militia who were attempting to harass Union ships. The handwriting is a bit shaky, as though the young sailor experienced bouncing waves. On May 18, he recounts seeing several men riding the beach on horseback near the Cape Henry Lighthouse, "and you could see another fellow shaking his fist as if he was impressing something upon the others." At noon on May 22, they "hauled close to the beach and fired the first offensive shot at the wagons and horsemen."

"Gosh, can you imagine, being eighteen he must have been full of ginger," says Ferguson. On one wall of her living room in the Nimmo section of Virginia Beach are photos of her late husband, who retired from the navy as master chief; her father, who flew as a pilot in World War I; and her son, who is now a deputy under secretary of defense. Beside the photos is a framed letter from her father's father, who was wounded at Gettysburg. And, finally, tucked in a folder is a faded photo of her mother's father, Farrell. In spite of the condition of the image, he looks dashing with his neatly trimmed mustache.

The opening salvo from the *Quaker City* became a running battle that would go on for weeks. An item appeared in the *New York Times* on June 16, 1861, quoting the *Norfolk Day Book*:

> The steamer Quaker City *captured a schooner off the Capes and carried her into the Roads. She returned about 4 o'clock that afternoon, and opened fire upon the Princess Anne Cavalry, stationed on Cape Henry Beach. She fired six shots at the quarters, none of which took effect except in the pine trees…The Cavalry Captain, John Fentress, is daily exposed to the fire of the steamer, but so far, fortunately, no one has been hurt.*

The *Day Book* goes on to lament the lack of heavy cannon on the beach with which "this steamer could easily be sunk from the position she takes to annoy our troops on the beach."

Captain Fentress served alongside his three sons in the Princess Anne Cavalry. All of them survived the war. One of the sons, Thomas, a doctor, represented Princess Anne County in the Virginia General Assembly after the war. Another, John, who was wounded in 1864, was the great-great-grandfather of Gary Fentress, Virginia Beach's deputy city attorney. And it further turns out that while Fentress was council to Virginia Beach's Planning Commission, Ferguson served as a member of the commission.

Needless to say, they kidded each other about a time when their relatives did everything they could—fortunately without success—to kill each other.

Norwegian Lady

They were *so* close. After a journey of more than one thousand miles, the Norwegian bark *Dictator* and its passengers and crew, including the wife and son of the captain, were near enough to the relative shelter of the Chesapeake Bay that they might have seen Cape Henry Light. That is, if a raging storm hadn't blinded them.

The aging 191-foot wooden vessel had been hammered by severe storms almost from the time it left Pensacola three weeks earlier. Now this: torrential rain, fifty-four-mile-an-hour northeasterly winds and towering seas that drove the ship ever closer to the Virginia Beach coastline. Ten fathoms, six, four and a half! And then the sandbar, 350 yards off the beach.

It was Good Friday morning, March 27, 1891.

Upstairs in the Old Coast Guard Station at the Virginia Beach Oceanfront is a display case for the ill-fated *Dictator.* Among the artifacts are a ship's bell, a decorative lion's head from the ship's stern, an engraved pearl-handled butter knife and an unrecognizable hunk of pedestal that is all that's left of the ship's original figurehead.

There's also a photo of a portion of the hull that washed up on the beach and a faded picture of ten surviving crew members standing in front of the former Seatack Life-Saving Station. Among them is the forlorn captain, Jorgen M. Jorgensen, his hands clasped in front. Regrettably, absent from the grainy image is his wife, Johanne Pauline ("Paua") Jorgensen, and their four-year-old son, Carl. This was the most poignant part of what we think of as the tragedy of the Norwegian Lady.

According to *The Norwegian Lady and the Wreck of the Dictator* by William O. Foss of Virginia Beach, a series of incidents doomed the ship. Most of the *Dictator*'s lifeboats were destroyed by a falling mast. Breeches buoys—which carried passengers ashore in pants-like slings—didn't reach the stricken ship because cannons that propelled them couldn't fire into the howling wind. And the lifesaving team leader, in spite of angry protests from onlookers, refused to risk the lives of his crew by sending boats into the surf. (He would later lose his job over this.) Still, a single remaining lifeboat made it ashore. A lifeline hauled to the ship made it possible for a few others to make it to safety.

But as Captain Jorgensen attempted to get his wife and child into a rescue sling, the ship began breaking apart. In a desperate attempt, he grasped a heavy ladder and tried to float the three of them to safety, but the ladder got away in the waves. The boy, lashed to him, was torn away by heavy seas and his wife was washed overboard and drowned. The grief-stricken and half-drowned captain washed up on the beach.

All told, seven were lost. Johanne and Carl Jorgensen's bodies were recovered and buried in Norfolk's Elmwood Cemetery. A fading inscription on the back of the headstone says, "*Lenge Leve Din Minde. Hvil I Fred.* Long live your memory. Rest in Peace."

The day after the shipwreck, the manager of the Princess Anne Hotel took a guest for a ride on the beach in a buckboard and discovered a large wooden object rolling in the surf. It was the figurehead from the *Dictator*, a "woman of heroic proportions draped in classic garments," as Foss put it.

The figurehead, the original Norwegian Lady, was placed on a pedestal in front of the hotel at Sixteenth Street, where it remained for sixty years until weather and souvenir collectors consumed it. In September 1962, in joint ceremonies in Virginia Beach and the oceanfront town of Moss, Norway, identical nine-foot bronze statues, monuments to sailors at sea, were unveiled.

I AM
THE NORWEGIAN LADY
I STAND HERE
AS MY SISTER BEFORE ME
TO WISH ALL MEN OF THE SEA
SAFE RETURN HOME

Footnote: The yellow pine timber that had been the ship's cargo washed up on shore and was eventually used for the interior of St. Luke's Church in Norfolk. The congregation merged with Christ Church to form Christ & St. Luke's Episcopal Church.

A Dapper Man

The Sargeant Memorial Room at Norfolk Public Library celebrated that history collection's eightieth birthday recently, a tribute to the dapper, genial man who started the library and gave the city a key to its history. William Henry Sargeant, a former teacher, librarian and bookseller in Baltimore, became Norfolk's first head librarian in 1895. It was a difficult period for the library. The local library association, which charged fees for its services, was on the verge of bankruptcy when a group of "gentlemen," as a newspaper account put it, paid off its debts and hired Sargeant to run a public library.

Sargeant did well. He "has seen the rise of the Norfolk Public Library from an insignificant affair to one of the most important of the intellectual institutions of the city," reported *The Norfolk Landmark* on November 12, 1911.

He was fascinated by local history and saw how fast things were changing as tree-lined residential neighborhoods gave way to a downtown commercial district. In 1897, he began collecting maps, documents and photographs that would capture and preserve what seemed to be changing before his eyes. He also focused on "Virginiana," all things important to Virginia history.

Ten years after his death in 1917, Mary Pretlow, the new head librarian, realized that the library needed a history room and got it started. Among the first items collected were his papers and books.

The SMR is a beehive of history books, scrapbooks, cemetery records, vital records, church records, court records, ships' passenger lists, photographs, rare first editions and just about everything else you ever wanted to know about Norfolk history and, not surprisingly, the state and region. It is, hands down, one of the finest local history and genealogical collections in the state.

Right: Photograph of the genial and dapper William Henry Sargeant, Norfolk's first head librarian. *Courtesy of the Sargeant Memorial Room, Norfolk Public Library.*

Below: Norfolk Harbor, 1856, artist unknown. *Courtesy of the Sargeant Memorial Room, Norfolk Public Library.*

CITY AND HARBOR OF NORFOLK, VIRGINIA, 1856.

Thanks to George Tucker, who must have begun writing this column before Sargeant came to town, thousands of photographs that the *Pilot* once almost threw away were saved. They now make up the bulk of about sixty-five thousand photos, all neatly filed with serial numbers, in the collection. Thousands of them have been scanned and hundreds made available online at www.npl.lib.va.us.

But we know little else about Sargeant. His obituary from March 23, 1917, says he was born in Morristown, New Jersey, in 1842 and that his parents moved to Baltimore, where his father became an eminent Episcopal clergyman and educator. The obit also contains a clue as to how he got here. In 1873, he married Elizabeth Williams, "daughter of Horatio N. Williams of Norfolk." They moved to a country home outside Norfolk in 1876 and then to York Street in the city.

So who was she and how did they meet? Here's where history comes around full circle. Norfolk city historian Peggy McPhillips, poring over reference material in the very SMR that William Henry Sargeant inspired—city directories, census records, newspaper files, birth and death notices and the like—found some intriguing answers about part of the man's life.

Elizabeth Williams was ten when her father, a merchant from Massachusetts, died in 1953. It is not known what became of her mother, Phoebe, but census records for 1860 show that seventeen-year-old Elizabeth was living with one Martha O'Brien, who ran a business making women's clothing, specifically "mantuas," a type of loose-fitting gown. Shortly after that, this region was thrown into the turmoil of the Civil War, and it is likely, McPhillips says, that Elizabeth went to Baltimore to learn a trade. And there she met our hero.

A wonderful Sargeant nugget comes from a *Ledger-Dispatch* clipping from 1911, saying that burglars entered the library, then on Freemason Street, and made off with five dollars and half a box of fine cigars, "which the genial librarian, William Henry Sargeant Sr., is famous for handing out to his friends."

How do we know he was dapper? Look at the accompanying photo that shows him wearing a straw boater hat and neatly trimmed beard. "Looks like someone you'd like to know," says McPhillips.

IN BROAD DAYLIGHT

TRAGEDY IN THE HEART OF CITY
Charles J. Cannon Shot Down by Police Captain Prince
SAYS HE WAS JUSTIFIED

Those were the headlines that newspaper readers saw in the morning paper of August 4, 1900. They must have gasped as the type jumped off the page and then read the details with fascination bordering on disbelief.

In an alleyway between the customshouse and Citizens Bank on Main Street, Captain Michael H. Prince had confronted Charley Cannon, his lifelong friend. The two stood, each with one arm on the other's shoulder. Prince had been the best man in Cannon's wedding and Cannon was the godfather to one of Prince's children. Their conversation was brief and soon turned angry. Suddenly Prince pulled a gun from his jacket pocket and shot Cannon several times. Then, as Cannon lay in agony on the ground, Prince walked up to him, leaned over and shot him in the head.

Prince surrendered his pistol to a nearby police officer and walked to the station house, where he told his boss, the chief of police, "I am your prisoner. I shot Charley Cannon."

The slaying of Cannon, an oyster inspector and saloonkeeper, was witnessed by dozens of people in broad daylight. The preliminary hearing on August 4—the same day as Cannon's funeral at St. Mary's Catholic Church—was held right next to the scene of the murder, the customshouse. But the trial—it was a federal case because the assault took place on U.S. property—was to be the first major criminal case held in the marble-clad courtroom in the new federal building on Plume Street. The building would later become home of the Norfolk Public Library's downtown branch.

It was one of the most sensational murder trials ever witnessed in the city, conducted by some of the most prominent prosecutors and attorneys in the region. Fascinated citizens packed the courtroom, hanging on every word, gasping at each new revelation as witnesses, and Prince himself, took the stand.

At the arraignment on December 10, Prince, age forty-two, stood with downcast eyes, shifting his weight. Several times he sighed deeply, but when asked how he responded to the charges, his voice was firm. "Not guilty."

The trial took place before Judge Edmund Waddill. Edgar Allan, a bulldog of a district attorney from Richmond, served as prosecutor. Prince was represented by local attorneys R.R. Thorpe and T.H. Willcox. The latter was a former judge and founding partner in what became one of Norfolk's largest law firms, Willcox & Savage.

The prosecution put numerous witnesses on the stand. It established beyond doubt that Prince shot Cannon. But whether he had done it coolly and deliberately or in a moment of temporary madness would be for the jury to decide. The first witness to cause a stir in the courtroom was Mrs. Charles J. Cannon. She appeared to be in deep mourning, with a long black veil pushed back from her sad face. She was, she said, Cannon's widow and now "I have five helpless children."

But her appearance provided an opening for the defense. Willcox showed her an anonymous note, and after first denying it, she confessed she had written it to Prince. The note said, "Mike, I don't like to have anything to do with a man and wife, but I think it a damn shame the way that your wife is treating you." She suggested that he "make it your business" to go to Plume Street at night "and watch her going down there to meet a married man... and when you see her with this man you beat her like hell."

Who was the married man? When the defense put on its case, it quickly became clear that it was Prince's old friend Charley Cannon.

When Prince took the stand, he was pale and his voice was shaky. On August 1, he said, he had noticed that his wife was trying to conceal a letter and grabbed it from her. It was to Cannon. "C. Send me $10. I am in more trouble than I ever was in my life. I will tell you all when I see you."

Prince testified that Cannon's wife told him, "Your wife and my Charley are being intimate." When he confronted her, he said, she confessed to the affair. He saw his old friend downtown and asked if it were true, and "I told him I had received letters and positive information that he had been going with my wife. He said, in a sort of sneering manner, 'I am not the only man.'"

Prince claimed that he had no intention of killing Cannon, but that comment enraged him and he reached for his pistol. He had not, he said, taken any action for his children's sake. And at that point, he slumped forward, his face in his hands, and wept. Finally, he was able to say, "I struggled hard to save my children this terrible disgrace."

After six days of trial, the prosecution and defense rested their cases.

If ever it could be said that a hush fell over a courtroom, the one that descended on the grand marble chamber in the federal building on Plume Street must have been total as Police Captain Michael H. Prince rose to face the jury. And if anyone could be said to look pale as a ghost, it was he. If convicted, he would go to the gallows. Either way, it seemed, he was a ruined man.

"Put yourself in this man's place," suggested R.R. Thorpe, a defense attorney who may have set an all-time record for what reporters used to call peroration.

> *See him drenched in the gall and wormwood of a tribulation the depth of which no mortal can fathom...Distracted between contending emotions: wishing to save his children the terrible disgrace, he meets...the corrupter of his wife, the violator of his bed. He meets this slimy reprobate, the hypocrite friend, when his brain was on fire and every fiend of hell was let loose upon his heart. What could he do? But one course was open to him. Kill himself or kill the vile author of his ruin.*

Among the Ten Commandments' "thou shalts" is one about killing, Thorpe points out, but there are two other prohibitions that apply: coveting a neighbor's wife and committing adultery.

"Michael H. Prince did what was right. He did what a sane man should have done and what an insane man could not have helped doing. Put that down, Mr. District Attorney, as my opinion. God put him in that frame of mind and made him do as he did."

The district attorney, Edgar Allan, sought to sow doubt in the jurors' minds, pointing to a note that Mrs. Prince had sent to Cannon, pleading for money to help feed her children. Allan said,

> *I don't know where Prince spent his money. There are no witnesses to show he cared a thing for his wife. There is no evidence to show a happy home was destroyed.*
>
> *They say he was wild when he shot. Every shot struck its mark. Think of it! A wild man, a crazy man, who fires five shots and the ground doesn't get a bullet unless it went through the body. He shot with such unerring aim that every bullet struck its victim...[then] this sick man walked*

M. H. PRINCE.

Michael Prince, a police captain, shot his lifelong friend during a jealous rage near the courthouse where he would be tried for murder. *Sketch from the* Norfolk Register, *December 15, 1900.*

deliberately back, took aim, stooped a little and fired and the blood oozed from the head, stopped the heartbeat and impulse and stopped Cannon's last prayer, "God be merciful to me, a sinner."

The killing of Cannon was clearly carried out with malice and forethought, Allan concluded. "I have done my duty as best I could, gentlemen of the jury, will you do yours?"

Prince trembled as he rose and faced the jury. "Gentlemen," said the clerk of court, "look upon the prisoner and say be he guilty or not guilty."

"Not guilty," the foreman said.

The spectators, many of whom apparently sided with Prince, burst into applause and cheering. After much shaking of hands, Prince walked from the court a free man, stopping first at his brother's cigar store and then taking a carriage to his mother's house on Granby Street. And then he vanished, at least from the public's eye. But descendants of both killer and victim have recently crossed paths and begun piecing the story together.

If ever there were closer friends than Mike Prince, once a captain in the Norfolk Police Department, and Charley Cannon, a prominent politician and saloonkeeper, they'd be hard to find. But Prince, apparently in a jealous rage, gunned down Cannon in broad daylight in downtown Norfolk on August 3, 1900.

A number of Cannon and Prince descendants—there are many here —have offered insights into the lives of their not-so-distant relatives. After more than a century, time seems to have healed most, but not all, of the hurt caused by the tragedy.

One might assume that, with infidelity tainting their marriage, the Princes would have parted company. Their children had been staying with Mike's brother while Mike waited in prison for the trial. His wife "is said to be residing with her father," *The Virginian-Pilot* said. A clear separation? But William T. Prince, a U.S. magistrate judge in Norfolk, contacted me.

He wrote in an e-mail,

> *It appears that Mike and Capitola, his wife, did not divorce. In fact, their daughter Lillian was born in 1904. Cappy died in 1933, Mike in 1934. They are buried side by side in St. Mary's Cemetery directly across a small lane from the graves of my parents. At Cappy's death she was identified as the wife of Michael; and at his death he was identified as the widower of Capitola.*
>
> *The Norfolk City Directory of 1910 lists "J.E. Prince & Co." as a wholesale wines and liquors distributor located at 102–104 Commercial Place. The principals of the company were James E. and Michael H. Prince and Robert L. Boggs.*

Judge Prince's daughter, Sarah Pishko, is the owner of Prince Books, the downtown bookstore that adjoins the TowneBank building. Between that building, originally Citizens Bank, and the U.S. Customshouse is a parking lot where the fatal shots were fired. On the wall near the counter of the Prince Books café is an enlarged flier for the wine and liquor business. The cheapest items on the list were brands of rye and gin for $1.25 per gallon.

John Cannon of Chesapeake, a great-grandnephew of Charley, has done extensive research on the family and found that Charley's father, an Irish immigrant, joined the Confederate army in April 1862 only to desert a month later. Nevertheless, Charles became a successful businessman. He rented river bottomland in the Elizabeth River, where he dredged for oysters and owned a saloon on Plume Street.

One of the striking things about Cannon's death was the testimony that he had been having an affair with Prince's wife, but the trial also revealed that she had gone to Cannon out of desperation because Prince wasn't bringing home enough money to support his growing family of seven children. "Mike was not a very good provider," says the present-day Cannon. "Capitola went to Charley's saloon to get money."

Was the outrage sparked by embarrassment that his wife was pleading for money to support her children rather than by a love affair?

John Cannon's cousin, Cheryl Cannon Hummer, also of Chesapeake, wrote that the two had talked about the tragedy many times "and have a hard time believing it was a crime of passion. It all sounded rather cold-blooded to us."

That being said, there might have been something of a wild streak in Cannon that was passed down from his father, who frequently showed up in court records of the time, she says. And then there was Prince. John Cannon found that Prince remained on the police force long enough to be involved in an incident at a rooming house where a derelict was threatening others with a rifle. "Police stormed the place and Mike shot him. It appears he was quick on the trigger."

Cheryl Hummer says the obituary notice and description of Charley's funeral service were "heart wrenching." Charley's parents were married at St. Mary's Catholic Church and now the same church was needed for their first son's funeral service. "A very sad story all around," she feels.

Near the entrance to St. Mary's Catholic Cemetery on Church Street —not far from Prince's grave—is a brown marble obelisk making the graves of the Cannon family. Prominently etched in the marble is the inscription, "My Beloved Son/Charles J. Cannon/Aug. 6, 1860–Aug. 3, 1900."

Annie Cannon, Charley's widow, ran his saloon successfully for many years after his death and later moved to Washington, D.C. She was not buried in the Cannon plot.

Family fascination with the Prince-Cannon matter has led to research in the genealogical records at Norfolk Public Library's Sargeant Memorial Room—now in the library's new home in the old courthouse building. Robert B. Hitchings, the head of SMR, who alerted me to this fascinating story, recalls that descendants of the two men recently expressed an interest in coming in for further study.

A grin works its way around the corners of Hitchings's mouth. "I told them they're welcome, but please leave their weapons at the door."

The shooting took place in the area between Citizens Bank, the tall building on the right, and the U.S. Customshouse. *Courtesy of TowneBank.*

THE ROUGH RIDER
SAVES THE DAY

On April 26, 1907, a pleasant spring day hereabouts, a Victorian classic, *East Lynne*, was set to run at the Majestic Theater in downtown Norfolk. Steamboats were taking on passengers all over the waterfront. Electric trains were leaving on the half hour from the Princess Anne Hotel in Virginia Beach. Downtown hotels were overcrowded, some sleeping three to a room, at the outrageous sum of ten dollars a head. Virtually every store in town closed for the day.

It was a huge day, a day to celebrate America's 300th birthday. The region was still reeling from the Civil War and its aftermath but feeling a surge of economic might from its railroads and ports. There were train stations and hotels going up all over the place. The itch to celebrate, and celebrate big, was irresistible.

Unlike 2007's birthday bash, which spread out all over the region, the Jamestown Exposition would take place at a single spot, a vast stretch of undeveloped land jutting out into Hampton Roads known as Sewell's Point.

After delays caused by funding glitches, the infrastructure of a small city—including water and electric lines, roadways, sidewalks and a mile of piers along the Hampton Roads waterfront—were rushed into place. Railway spurs were run out to the grounds, as were trolley tracks and a new roadway, Jamestown Exposition Boulevard, later named Hampton Boulevard.

Twenty-two states erected grand exhibition halls, which would one day serve as "Admiral's Row" officers' quarters. There were numerous exposition buildings showing off the country's architectural, scientific and manufacturing prowess. There was a miniature railway, a Temple of Mirth, a "Shoot the Chute" ride, Civil War cycloramas and a Wild West Show with cowboys, cowgirls, Indians and rancheros. You name it, we had it.

To top it off, Hampton Roads hosted the largest gathering of warships in history, including sixteen battleships, six destroyers, three cruisers and several smaller vessels, accompanied by more than a dozen foreign ships.

There were celebrities aplenty, but the star of the show was the Rough Rider himself, President Teddy Roosevelt. He made the trip down from Washington on a yacht and, passing through the fleet, received thunderous greetings. Hampton Roads must have been thick with smoke from the rolling salutes. Then, as he stepped onto the new piers, the huzzahs of the crowd rivaled the roar of the guns.

An estimated crowd of sixty thousand looked on, including heads of state, foreign diplomats and celebrities. T.R. made a typically bully and expansive speech, welcoming visitors from around the world. "They have come to assist us in celebrating what was in very truth the birthday of this nation," he declared.

But what the history books seldom mention is that Roosevelt's visit nearly resulted in tragedy. Microfilm from *The Virginian-Pilot*—the merger of the two names took place in 1898—flies across the reader, revealing exhaustive

President Theodore Roosevelt speaking at the dedication of the Jamestown Exposition in 1907. *Courtesy of the Sargeant Memorial Room, Norfolk Public Library.*

coverage of the day of and the day after the event. It includes not just the speech but also the tension-filled moments leading up to it.

After the anthems, prayers and introductions, the huge crowd began pressing toward the reviewing stand where Roosevelt had taken the stage. There weren't loudspeakers in those days, and people strained to hear the president above what had become a howling wind. The result was that those closest to the platform were in danger of being trampled.

The hero of San Juan Hill literally leaped to the rescue. "With the agility of a schoolboy," the paper said, Roosevelt jumped onto a small, somewhat shaky table, waved his arms and cried out to the multitude to remember that there were women and children in the front row, and "if you keep pushing forward you are going to hurt them."

The commander in chief shouted orders to the leader of a squad of mounted cavalrymen who were brought in to break up the crowd, and quickly the situation calmed. "Roosevelt had saved the day," the newspaper declared.

Later, in a letter to his son Kermit, the president reported only that he had "made the usual speech, held the usual reception, went to the usual lunch, etc., etc."

HOUSE OF MEMORIES

In Katharine Ashman's closet are three dresses that her grandmother, Annie Esther Todd Wool, wore one hundred years ago to numerous extravagant functions at the Jamestown Exposition. She holds up one of them, a floor-length pink satin dress with lace top and train. "My grandmother was so tiny that even as a ten-year-old I hardly fit in them," she says.

Ashman's condominium overlooking Linkhorn Bay in Virginia Beach contains other century-old memorabilia, including a framed invitation: "The officers and directors of the Jamestown Exposition request the honor of your presence on Friday the 26th of April 1907 at the formal opening of the Jamestown Tercentennial Exposition." It's addressed to her grandfather, Theodore J. Wool.

And then there's a framed photo showing family members arrayed about the wide porches of a great mansion not long after the exposition. Her grandparents lived in the North Carolina House, one of twenty-one buildings erected by various states for the 300th celebration of the Jamestown landing. Outside is a pony cart that was used by the five children, one of them her father. The house is now part of Admiral's Row at the world's largest naval installation, and her grandfather had a lot to do with its being there.

The investors who assembled the land at Sewell's Point went broke because of poor attendance at the lavish exposition. The land was taken over by Norfolk's Fidelity Land and Investment Corp., and the job fell to Wool, the firm's general counsel, to unload it.

Although he was born in Nyack, New York, Theodore Wool had strong tidewater ties. His father was a cousin of General John E. Wool, the fellow for whom Fort Wool was named. Shortly after the Civil War, the family moved to Petersburg, Virginia. After earning his degree at Hampden-Sydney

The North Carolina House was home to the family of Theodore J. Wool following the Jamestown Exposition. *Courtesy of Katharine Ashman.*

College, Wool became a public school principal in Portsmouth and married the petite "Essie" Todd. A law degree followed, as did practices in Norfolk and Portsmouth.

Selling the exposition's 473 acres was not an easy job, but Wool had one buyer in mind—the U.S. Navy. There were numerous other naval operations here, including the navy yard and hospital at Portsmouth, and the area was already blessed with deep harbors and channels, so it seemed natural to establish a base here. Still, negotiations went on for nine years until Congress declared war on Germany in 1917.

Almost immediately, money was approved to buy the land and build piers, aviation facilities, a submarine base, a hospital and recruit training station. Soon, eight million yards of mud were dredged from the western side of Sewell's Point to provide for deep-water piers—and the spoil from that operation just about doubled the size of the base. Secretary of the Navy Josephus Daniels declared that it would become "the most ideal naval operating base in the world."

Ground was broken on Independence Day 1917. An account in the newspaper that day says that contractors would begin work immediately.

"Work on a larger scale than has ever been undertaken in this section will start with a rush at New Jamestown tomorrow morning."

And the fortunes of Norfolk would be drastically changed, thanks in large part to the persistence of the former Portsmouth principal.

Theodore and Esther Wool didn't stay long in the stately mansion on Sewell's Point. It was simply too isolated and distant from the amenities of Norfolk. They moved to Colonial Avenue in Ghent, not far from where their granddaughter Katharine grew up.

She remembers going downtown to her grandfather's office and walking with him to the Ames & Brownley Department Store for lunch in the tearoom. And recently she discovered her kindergarten report card from the Williams School that includes a note: "I am pleased at this excellent first report of our little Katharine and feel sure she will continue to take interest in her school work. Feb. 19, 1938. T.J. Wool."

Other than the fact that the navy base is on the grounds of the exposition, few people know all the effort that went into its creation, Ashman feels. For her, having the mementoes keeps the memory alive.

"I've been proud of it all my life."

SOUNDING THE ALARM

Before dawn, June 10, 1907. A young man from Richmond rubs the sleep from his eyes as he hustles to the train station near his cottage on the Virginia Beach oceanfront. He's on his way to join members of a military unit that is to escort President Theodore Roosevelt during Georgia Day celebrations at the Jamestown Exposition.

But something catches his attention, smoke and, yes, a small flame, spurting from the kitchen of the hotel where the train station stands. He rushes into the building and, failing to find a bucket and water, alerts the cook. Together they run from room to room of the four-story hotel, frantically banging on doors and sounding the alarm. Other employees join the effort. The building is wood, tinder dry. In minutes the entire structure is engulfed in flames.

A brief flashback: it had only been a couple of decades since the first attempts were made to bring people across the farmlands, swamps and forests to the beach. In 1880, several Norfolk business tycoons built the Virginia Beach Hotel and formed the Norfolk, Virginia Beach & Southern Railroad to provide rail service from Norfolk to the oceanfront.

The hotel was sold, remodeled and reopened in 1887 as the Princess Anne Hotel and soon became known as one of the country's poshest resorts, where the rich and famous could luxuriate at the beach, soak in salt baths and dance the night away. One newspaper, *The Norfolk Landmark*, called it "the social centre of the summer colony of Virginia Beach."

When the exposition opened in the spring of 1907, the railroad, now Norfolk and Southern, offered trolley service there from the hotel every thirty minutes for twelve and a half cents each way. It is on the first trolley of the day that the young man is due to depart when he spots the fire.

Visitors to Virginia Beach pose in front of the Princess Anne Hotel in 1887. *Courtesy of* The Virginian-Pilot.

There's a frantic scramble as guests, mostly in sleepwear, many carrying children, flee from their rooms. They huddle outside as flames begin to envelop the building and they realize, to their horror, that a maid who had helped sound the alarm is trapped on the roof and quickly overcome. She and one of the hotel clerks are lost in the fire.

The hotel manager, who at first thought the contents of the safe, including the day's receipts, were lost, twice faints from his grief. Witnesses see a "half-crazed man waving his hands above his head," reported *The Virginian-Pilot*. Members of his family carry him to a nearby cottage and put him to bed.

Meanwhile, the crowd realizes that the conflagration may jump to the other buildings along the beach. Dozens of them, including many women from the hotel still dressed in "night clothes," form a bucket brigade, dipping water from the ocean and passing it along to others who douse the next-door O'Keefe's Hotel and keep the fire from spreading to other nearby buildings and cottages. Except for the two hotel employees, all others are saved.

Two hours after the fire is discovered, the once fashionable hostelry is a charred mass, victim of a defective flue in the kitchen. Four red brick chimneys mark the spot where the hotel once stood. Although officials say the hotel will quickly be rebuilt, it is not for another twenty years that a new luxury hotel that might equal the first, the Cavalier, rises.

It is not known whether the young man from Richmond was ever able to join his field artillery unit later that day and take part in the booming salute given the president as he disembarked from his yacht at the exposition

Bathers and lifeguard at Virginia Beach, 1920s. *Courtesy of* The Virginian-Pilot.

grounds. It seems unlikely because he was overcome by smoke and had to be carried from the burning building.

But it is certain that his actions on that spring morning averted a major tragedy and possibly saved the young village of Virginia Beach.

GREAT WHITE DISPLAY
OF MIGHT

A warm, cloudy, century-ago morning. Thousands of people, wives, children, sisters and sweethearts, mob the shoreline and pier at Old Point Comfort and the ramparts at Fort Monroe. Thousands more watch from excursion steamers out on Hampton Roads or clamber onto trains heading to Cape Henry.

Just after 8:00 a.m., the presidential yacht *Mayflower*, with Teddy Roosevelt onboard, arrives after an all-night journey from Washington and the roadstead erupts in thunderous salutes that can be heard from miles away.

"Did you ever see such a fleet?" the president exclaims. "And such a day! Isn't it magnificent? Oughtn't we all to feel proud?" And later, he is heard to say, "I tell you our enlisted men are everything. They are perfectly bully and they are up to everything required of them. This is indeed a great fleet and a great day!"

On the decks of sixteen white-hulled battleships, ceremonial flags are dropped and from their mastheads signals are flashed. "Ready." "Get underway." And, without further ado, the ships weigh anchor. A band on the quarterdeck of the yacht strikes up "The Girl I Left Behind" and "The Star-Spangled Banner" as the ships pass by and steam out toward the Virginia Capes, clouds of black smoke trailing aft in the stiff breeze.

It was a heady occasion for a president who, twelve months before, had received the Nobel Peace Prize for brokering the end of war between Russia and Japan. Now he was launching a chest-thumping demonstration of American sea power to convince the world that the United States had the will and the means to back up its diplomacy.

And it worked.

According to the Naval Historical Center, the main goal of the cruise was to demonstrate to Japan that America could easily shift its sea power

A great fleet of white-painted warships departs from Hampton Roads to display America's flag around the world. *Courtesy of the Mariners' Museum.*

from the Atlantic to the Pacific. Despite the Treaty of Portsmouth, as the agreement between the two warring countries was called, the Japanese were still restless and threatening to invade the Philippines. A little big-stick, gunboat diplomacy was called for.

So off they went on that auspicious morning. The sixteen coal-burning battleships, with fourteen thousand sailors and marines aboard, turned south after passing the capes and began an extraordinary forty-three-thousand-mile journey around the world. They would sail all the way around South America and put in at twenty ports of call on six continents, receiving carnival-like greetings at many of them.

The only serious incident occurred in Rio, where a ballroom brawl between sailors and longshoremen turned into a bottle- and brick-throwing donnybrook. But most receptions were peaceful and enthusiastic, including the one in Tokyo. Schoolchildren sang "Hail Columbia" and citizens honored the fleet with a torchlight parade. Most importantly, the appearance led to a treaty that, temporarily at least, quelled Japan's ambitions. Roosevelt would later declare that the cruise was his most important contribution toward peace.

The battlewagon procession continued through the Suez Canal to the Mediterranean and, once again, the Atlantic. After a fourteen-month odyssey, on a rainy February 22, 1909, the Great White Fleet returned to Hampton Roads with, again, cheering multitudes onshore and twenty-one-gun salutes. Among the tunes played by shipboard bands was a happy version of "There's No Place Like Home."

After the welcoming, the battleships, now besmirched with grime and coal residue, proceeded directly to Norfolk Naval Shipyard, where they received coats of the navy's now official ship color, battleship gray.

MEETING BY CHANCE

This is a story that begins in the memory of a lovely man, then approaching four score years, tapping on his typewriter as scenes of his youth raced through his mind.

As a lad of eleven, he began spending summer vacations at sea with his grandfather, Ben Correll. The old sea captain would carry coal from Whitehaven, their homeplace on the coast of England, to port cities along the Irish coast. Some of the passages were stormy enough to banish all thoughts of a career at sea from his mind. But then again, there was the midnight watch when he first took a turn at the helm.

The second mate had gone below to make tea and left him there, his hands clammy with excitement and fear. But after a short while, holding a steady course under a three-quarter moon in a gentle breeze, he didn't want to be relieved, not then and not for the rest of the four-hour watch.

"I was spellbound, complete and unalloyed pleasure possessed me, I felt a keen sense of the beauty and loveliness that was all around me," he wrote. Seals gamboled in the wake of the ship as it keeled over slightly, "her sails billowed by the filling winds, the old and faithful tub answering with accuracy every touch of the helm."

The memoir was written by my grandfather, James Dunlop. It adds richness—in some parts complete with lengthy passages of Scottish-Irish dialect—to what I know of my ancestors. The amazing thing to me is how the strands of his story interweave with one another. My mother, Elizabeth Correll Clancy, sat down with me and a video camera a couple of years ago and told me the story of her grandfather, Mortimer Horton, descendant of a family that settled on Long Island in the early 1600s. There's a landmark in Cutchogue known as Horton House.

Foursome on their honeymoon in 1910: Bob and Ada Milne, Mimi and Jim Dunlop. *Courtesy of Joan Syms.*

Mortimer Horton seemed to have it made, a prominent lawyer who lived just across from New York City in then fashionable Hoboken, New Jersey, with a wife and three children, a horse and carriage and all the trappings of the good life. Maybe too much of the good life.

"I believe my grandfather Mortimer led quite an interesting life," my mother said.

When he passed away suddenly at age forty-two from appendicitis, his family discovered that his frequent trips into the city in the company of the high-rolling and famously gluttonous "Diamond Jim" Brady—I love this part—left him not rich but in fact deeply in debt.

So his widow, Katarina, did what she had to do. She took in sewing and opened up the spacious house to boarders. And who should come live there but James Dunlop, who had not, after all, taken up the call of the sea.

Grandpa Jim and coworker Bob Milne had made their way to America to work for Postal Telegraph Cable, one of the world's growing new communications companies. Searching for good but affordable lodgings, they both took rooms at the house in Hoboken and promptly, it seems, fell in love with the two daughters.

Jim and Bob married Mimi and Ada Horton on the same day in 1910. Both families moved to Brooklyn and raised a combined total of five daughters. One of them, Kay, died in Boston at the age of ninety-six. Her kid sister, Elizabeth, born in 1915, moved to Norfolk, where she would be close to her son and two of many great-grandchildren.

One of the things that occurred to her in telling the story of her family was how lucky she is that her grandfather went broke. "I wouldn't have had my wonderful dad," she said with a smile.

And you would not have just read this column.

HIDDEN TREASURE

You're in the family shelter of the Union Mission Building in downtown Norfolk, looking up through the open ceiling of a closet. Light from your flashlight plays across images of genteel folk standing on a shoreline and looking seaward. At first, you can't tell what they're looking at; they seem to be gesturing toward something on the water. So you ask for a ladder, climb up though the opening and splash the light around the walls.

And then your breath catches. What you're looking at are long-hidden scenes from our past.

The ladies and gentlemen on this canvas are watching the second battle of Hampton Roads, the duel of the ironclads *Virginia* and *Monitor*. Then, as your light plays around the vast open room that's hidden by temporary partitions and a false ceiling, you realize there are not just a dozen or so full-length murals, each depicting part of Virginia's past. This place is a museum.

Since 1972, the Union Mission has occupied one of the most historic buildings in the city, the Navy YMCA, built with funds donated by John D. Rockefeller. Not John D. Jr. Not David. Not Nelson or Jay, but the famous industrialist himself. A bronze plaque just inside the entrance proclaims that the gift was "a tribute to the brave men of the Navy."

The six-story Beaux Arts building at the corner of Brooke Avenue and Boush Street opened its doors on March 17, 1909, and went on to become a second home for thousands of sailors through two world wars. Originally, they could rent cots for seventy-five cents a night and private rooms for two dollars. They could swim in a pool, work out in a gym, play pool, eat in a dining room, get a haircut, bring their dates to dances and, at least temporarily, forget about going off to war.

The Navy Y was a downtown fixture during an era when the city swarmed with white uniforms. It literally overflowed with guests. Sailors could be found sleeping on chairs and tables, even in phone booths. There were thousands of weddings in the chapel, with a record 368 alone in 1944. There were dances, square dances and Saturday night stage shows. An estimate in *The Virginian-Pilot* held that, between Pearl Harbor and the Japanese surrender, more than sixteen million guests passed through its doors.

Artists prepare murals for the downtown Navy YMCA, built with funds given by John D. Rockefeller in 1909. *Courtesy of the Sargeant Memorial Room, Norfolk Public Library.*

The building seems to echo with memories. On a roof-to-basement tour with Linda Jones, public relations director for Union Mission, I wonder about the sailors who might have splashed in the tile-lined pool before heading off to war. "Leave your locker keys in slot," says a sign stenciled above one of the doors. Or maybe they played basketball in the gym where mercury vapor lights can still be coaxed on, or ran around the elevated track. Shot pool in the room that is now a chapel. Caught a few hours' sleep in the narrow rooms flooded with sunlight. Stood on the roof deck, with its commanding view of the harbor, and watched ferries, steamers and ships passing in the night.

Now, another era for the ninety-nine-year-old building approaches as Union Mission prepares to leave for its new location on Virginia Beach Boulevard, bolstered by a $12 million capital campaign. The building and adjacent parking lot, both owned by the shelter, are for sale. The only interest shown so far, Harvey Lindsay, the listing agent, tells me, is for condos or apartments, "but so far nothing's been worked out." One thing Lindsay is clear about: "I wouldn't be a party to turning it over to anybody who would try to tear it down."

Still, the landmark building is considered endangered and, like other structures in downtown, could face the wrecking ball. A lot depends on the market for in-town residences, or perhaps the will to preserve it. One idea that Norfolk Historical Society president Louis Guy floated recently is to use the building for a new downtown library. It would be a huge undertaking, but certainly a dignified new beginning for a place with so much history. Whatever the use, he says, "We can't afford to lose it. If it's done right, it could be another downtown treasure."

Recently, I went to the Kirn Library's local history room and found, in a file on the old Navy Y, a brochure with a couple of pictures that caught my eye: one of a dance in the ballroom, with those murals in the background; another, taken shortly before the opening, of a group of New York artists putting the final touches on the murals. They presented them as a gift to the city.

Does that gift, you may wonder, carry a covenant, unwritten and unspoken though it might have been, to preserve them and the space they occupy?

TOOTSIE

It was January 30, 1936, in Philadelphia when Tootsie Bashara, a twenty-one-year-old boxer from Norfolk, let his guard down in the first round and his opponent, world lightweight champ Tony Canzoneri, landed a vicious right uppercut. Bashara dropped to the canvas and stayed down for a nine-count. Then, in the third, after a hard left jab opened a cut in Bashara's eye, the fight and the dazzling boxing career of the "jawbreaker" from Lambert's Point were over.

Fred "Tootsie" Bashara began boxing at the age of fourteen. One of three boxing brothers, he was the most successful, winning, by one count, fifty-nine matches in a row. It was a time when "fistic warfare," as one newspaper called it, was enormously popular. The papers in the 1930s were full of stories about this or that match, all written glowingly about the top contenders in each weight class. So respectable were the fights of the era that many here were held as benefits for the Children's Clinic Athletic Association, an offshoot of what would become Children's Hospital of the King's Daughters.

Like other sports today, boxing was considered a way up the ladder, especially for inner-city immigrants. As Fred Bashara Jr., Tootsie's son, puts it, "In Norfolk during the Depression, if you didn't work at the shipyard, what did you do? A lot of guys went into fighting."

Tootsie's father, Habib, a circus strongman from Lebanon, had immigrated here illegally. At least there were no records showing his arrival. His growing family, with five daughters and five sons, lived at the abandoned Louisiana House at the Jamestown Exposition grounds until being forced out by the navy. Among Habib's many enterprises was a fruit stand on what was to become Hampton Boulevard.

"Tootsie" Bashara at the top of his career, about 1936. *Courtesy of Fred Bashara Jr.*

Fred Jr. runs an insurance agency on upper Colley Avenue not far from where his father, in later years, opened Tootsie's, a drive-up restaurant where beer was served at the curb. He showed me some of the many scrapbooks his father assembled, bulging with newspaper clippings and fight notices. His square-jawed, battered, but still handsome face fills the pages.

"Bashara never won any national titles," one story summed up, "but he fought some of the best in the game. Fighting in the lightweight class, the stocky slugger rose from a mere unknown amateur fighter to one of the leading boxers in the South."

Among the clippings is the account of how Tootsie broke the jaw of one opponent "with a series of right hand smashes," although his battered man somehow stayed on his feet through eight rounds.

But the limelight had a way of spoiling those unaccustomed to its glare. Tootsie was a "vicuna coat boxer," as his son puts it, a fast-living ladies' man who married at least five times. "When I was a little boy, I remember having footie pajamas on and my mother was standing at the door crying as my father went out for the night."

Loosely inserted in one of the scrapbooks is a 1931 contract in which Tootsie agreed to allow his manager, Carl Tranberger, to handle all money received for each fight except twenty dollars "for spending money." The manager would pay Tootsie's sister Marie five dollars a week for room and board and pay off his debts. "I further agree that I will not run any other bills unless satisfactory with Mr. Tranberger of whom I will first obtain consent."

He was at the top of his game, lightweight champion of Virginia, when Canzoneri's glove found his eye. His brother Tommy had lost an eye in the ring, and Tootsie, advised by a doctor that he could lose his, decided to hang it up. But he had already begun a second career as a professional golfer, and he soon took over as the golfing pro at a club in Elizabeth City. At one point he also ran a beer distributorship in Newport News.

One of his proudest accomplishments was arranging, with brother Tommy, a "Salute to Pearl Harbor" vaudeville and boxing show that raised more than $1 million in war bonds shortly after the start of World War II. He died in May 1994 at the age of eighty.

Fred Bashara didn't know his father well because Tootsie had left home when he was young. What had he left him, other than the ability to hit a speed bag? Well, maybe a lesson in how far grit and determination will get you.

Back when he was in the U.S. Air Force in Tacoma, Washington, Fred and some friends stopped by a bar where the walls were covered with pictures of boxers. When the bartender asked for an ID and recognized his name, he pointed to a photo and said, "Are you Tootsie's son?"

"My buddies and I had all the beer we wanted on the house and heard some great stories about the 'manly' sport," he said.

NO ONE WAS LAUGHING

Few saw it coming, although the morning paper of August 22, 1933, hinted of a menace heading this way. The National Weather Bureau issued a warning about a tropical disturbance near Bermuda, moving slowly west-northwest and "attended by dangerous gales." That morning, a driving storm dumped six inches of rain on local streets and sunk a tug out on Hampton Roads.

Later in the day, death came to Willoughby Bay. Two men who had gone out fishing attempted to return to shore in a skiff but lost one of their oars. Within seventy-five feet of land, the little boat began taking on water and one of the two, W. Oscar Dockery of Stockley Gardens, dove overboard and tried to tow them to safety. He was overcome by waves and drowned.

But the full force of the storm had not yet been felt, and few suspected what was coming. Norfolk-bound passenger steamers stuck to their schedules, departing from Baltimore and heading south. Late that afternoon, visitors to the oceanfront noticed a deathly calm, with an eerie orange glow in the sky. Guests at the Courtney Terrace Hotel on Sixteenth Street laughed, no doubt uneasily, as a dance band played "Stormy Weather."

No one was laughing the next morning. The storm made landfall north of Cape Hatteras and by 9:30 a.m. arrived with all its fury in Hampton Roads.

"The first warning we got was when the wind blew out the window in our room, which faced to the east, shattering glass over the bed in which my brother was asleep," Tren Brownley related in *Tales of the '33 Hurricane*, edited by C. Randolph Hudgins Jr. They quickly dressed and went to the hotel's living room, only to have a "tremendous wave" break through one wall of the room, setting furniture afloat. Amazingly, they found safety by climbing onto shelves in the hotel's linen storage room and waiting for the storm to pass.

The scene on Granby Street after the hurricane. *Photo by Charles Borjes of* The Virginian-Pilot, *courtesy of the Sargeant Memorial Room, Norfolk Public Library.*

A mom and dad sleeping in a cottage on Fifty-fifth Street were jolted awake by a door being torn off its hinges. They ran to the room where their baby boy, W. MacKenzie Jenkins Jr., was sleeping and found him partly submerged in water. Using the door as a raft, the father paddled his family, and later their dog, to high ground and safety.

They were lucky. The Great Chesapeake-Potomac Hurricane, as it would be called, took the lives of at least eight people locally, including a mother, daughter and bystander who stepped into a puddle where a power line had fallen in Portsmouth. Two crew members of Norfolk-bound steamer *Madison* were swept to their deaths by giant waves that crashed into the vessel's port side. Although part of its superstructure was destroyed and guest cabins wrecked, the ship was able to limp into port, disgorging thirty-seven haggard and traumatized passengers. There were tales of heroism as police, fire and Coast Guard crews rescued survivors from the upper floors of battered houses. Nurses in Portsmouth reported to work by rowboat.

The hurricane leveled or damaged hundreds of homes, inflicting what *The Virginian-Pilot* called "tremendous damage" to Virginia Beach, Ocean View,

Willoughby Spit and Buckroe Beach. Thousands of trees were uprooted and cities were left powerless. The amusement park at Ocean View was heavily damaged, the old wooden boardwalk was completely splintered and trolley tracks were covered by mountains of sand.

Recently, I went to see Tom Hall, a lifelong Ocean View resident, who was eight at the time of the hurricane. His father was a plumbing and heating contractor who was called out later in the day to shut off water and power to scores of homes. He took his son along.

"The thing I'll always remember is the waves that tore away the beach side of a four-story brick building," Hall said. "There was a bathtub, you know, the old style with four legs, three stories up. While I'm standing there, I look up and I see the bathtub fall three stories to the sand. For an eight-year-old, that was an awesome sight."

It would take months to rebuild, to dig out of the sand and rubble, to replace plate-glass windows, to restore the amusement park, to recover from injuries. As for the stories about what took place, they'd never be forgotten.

PORT OF EMBARKATION

At the end of World War I, the city that sprang up as the result of Collis P. Huntington's railroad and shipyard went into a financial swoon from which it would not recover until the dogs of war were again unleashed and human cargo by the thousands again trod the decks of troop transports.

With the outbreak of World War II, the Newport News Port of Embarkation was reactivated. The army again leased and expanded the city's C&O piers. Before war's end, Hampton Roads would bid farewell to 730,000 soldiers and welcome back nearly that many at war's end.

Needless to say, the local USO was constantly jumping. The peninsula swarmed with barracks and tent camps, and this time a new phenomenon, German and Italian prisoners of war—some 130,000 arrived and marched off to POW camps at Fort Eustis and several other places, including one near the James River Bridge.

Because of the lurking presence of German U-boats, Hampton Roads had the feel of an armed fortress. The Coast Guard placed submarine nets at the mouth of the bay and navy destroyers patrolled the coast. All of this played out as convoys of outward-bound ships, ever on guard against attack, stole away under cover of darkness. All the while, the shipyard was operating at full capacity. Between the main yard on the James River and its subsidiary in Wilmington, the shipyard turned out close to fifty vessels.

But this time when peace returned, Newport News did not again go into decline. The shipyard continued aircraft carrier projects, and Fort Eustis became the permanent home of the Army Transportation Corps. Camp Patrick Henry was converted to an airport and state hospital. And out on the James off Mulberry Island, the hulking carcasses of decommissioned merchant marine vessels, especially the *Liberty* and *Victory* ships that helped win the war, began to congregate. The "ghost fleet" grew to more than 140 at its peak and then began to dwindle as the dangerously leaky ships were, one by one, towed to scrap yards.

The shipyard scrambled for work after the war, even taking on such distinctly non-maritime projects as wind tunnels and water turbines for places like the Hoover Dam and Muscle Shoals. But the most exciting civilian project was the exquisitely beautiful super passenger liner, the SS *United States*. The 990-foot luxury liner, christened on June 23, 1951, had its sea trials off the Virginia Capes and then, on its maiden voyage, set the transatlantic record of three days, ten hours and forty minutes—an average speed of 35.5 knots!

Now the city that the shipyard and railroad built was ready for the next leap, but the question was, in which direction—and how far? There was growing sentiment to merge, and not just with the rapidly growing Warwick County suburbs but with next-door Hampton as well.

Could there be a super-city called Hampton Roads? Norfolk, for one, which considered itself part of Hampton Roads, nixed the idea, and it seemed to collapse as Hampton merged with Elizabeth City County and Phoebus. And then Warwick went its own way. The county that had enjoyed the rapid suburbanization caused by the growth of Newport News became the city of Warwick on July 15, 1952.

But Warwick's independence was not to last. Its own growth pangs—as well as the loyalty that many residents felt toward the neighboring city where

Soldiers march through the first Victory Arch after returning from Europe, April 13, 1919. *Courtesy of the Mariners' Museum.*

they worked—led to the mega-merger of Warwick and Newport News. Not only did Warwick lose its status as a city, but also its proud name, as voters chose to call the new entity Newport News. And so it was that on July 1, 1958, the new city, with O.J. Brittingham Jr. serving as mayor, was born. The former boundary at Sixty-fourth Street was extended all the way to the James City County line, encompassing six square miles and 113,000 residents. It would grow to nearly 200,000 by century's end.

If it's hard to visualize how the place that John Smith once called "Newports Newes" became a modern city, I recommend a walk through Victory Landing Park on the downtown waterfront. Chiseled at the top of the venerable Victory Arch, a successor of the one that welcomed back combatants of two world wars, is the poignant inscription, "Greetings with love to those who return, a triumph with tears for those who sleep."

That's where the heart of the old city once beat.

IN THE COMPANY
OF MEMORIES

G arland Eaton was working at Norfolk Naval Shipyard, helping convert oil tankers into mini aircraft carriers, when Pearl Harbor was attacked. "I was working in the shipyard one hot day on those hot steel decks, and we were watching the airplanes just wafting around up in the sky, and I said to my buddy, 'You know, we need to be *up there*! We don't need to be down here.' So we asked our leading man if we could get off that evening. He said, 'What do you want to do, go fishing?' I said, 'No, we want to go join the Air Corps.'"

This is Garland's voice, almost sixty-seven years later, from a transcript of a "History Day" gathering at the Senior Resource Center in Creeds. He's one of dozens of residents who have taken part in an oral history project that aims to capture memories of the past before they're lost.

Days after making the decision to volunteer, Garland found himself in the army, headed for pilot training. But the path seemed endless. First, there was training in Miami, then Cleveland and, finally, aviation school in San Antonio. All the schools, all the training and then a ruptured appendix delayed things more.

"I had just finished pre-flight school when Germany fell," he says. "They slowed down graduations and the cadet program was stalled."

One thing led to another, and finally he went to aircraft mechanics' school, which would lead to being a flight engineer on a B-29 Superfortress. It was a forty-eight-week course, and about ten weeks before graduation, Japan fell. Garland never got to be a pilot, navigator or flight engineer. He returned home to Pungo, met Shirley Jones from Great Bridge, married and raised a family. He bought a service station just down Princess Anne Road, sold it and became a firefighter at Oceana Naval Air Station until he retired thirty-three years ago.

Eaton, *far right*, and friends at a downtown Norfolk bar, circa 1942. *Courtesy of Garland Eaton.*

During their life together, Garland and Shirley traveled the country in a motor home, rambled the beach in one of his numerous beach buggies and amassed hundreds, maybe thousands, of photographs and home movies. What do you do with them, especially old slides, a closet full of albums, movies and slides?

Meanwhile, along comes the Senior Resource Center's history project, and Garland realizes that he's not only the keeper of his family's history, but Pungo's as well, or at least part of it. Just about everybody who knew about the old days there has gone. This fragile thing, the history of a place, rests with him and a few others.

We had coffee at his kitchen counter one morning. He said,

> *Pungo. A lot of people still don't know it today. When they talk about Pungo, they don't go back to the businesses that were here. A lot of 'em will go back to the potato graders and maybe the ice plant, but prior to that we raised tobacco down here. That didn't work out, so we went to potatoes, and we had a potato grader. We had a barrel factory—potatoes were put in barrels when they dug 'em instead of bags. We raised cotton at one point. We had a cotton gin, we had an ice plant. We had a barrel factory. All that had been in the history of Pungo and it's disappeared.*

Garland, age eighty-four, lives in a rambler he built in 1961. He lost his wife last year. For company he has memories.

> *My daddy had the route to drive the school bus to the old Charity School. That's long gone now, but he got a contract in '36, a three-year contract to furnish and drive the bus. Ninety dollars a month plus all expenses. He went over to South Norfolk and bought a '36 Ford chassis. Took that chassis over to Newport News to the Hackney Body Works. You've seen those green Hackney wagons? Well, they built his body on that chassis.*

He got to talking with some friends, who asked if he remembered when President Franklin Roosevelt went by motorcade to one of the early performances of *Lost Colony* at Manteo in August 1937. The route took him through Great Bridge, and hundreds lined it to get a glimpse. Garland's father went one better; he got up a group of people, twenty-five or thirty of them, and drove them all down in the bus. "I'll never forget that." He pours more coffee. "I wish I had a picture of that bus."

STRONG-WILLED
ADVENTURER

The ten-page letter from Paris was written in a strong, forward-sloping cursive, with words that seem to bump into the edge of the page as though impatient to tell their story.

It was April 16, 1919, and Mary Pretlow had just witnessed the cruel devastation of war. Traveling with soldier companions to Reims, a city in northern France that lay in ruins, she had stood on a moonlit night and gazed at the famous, partly wrecked thirteenth-century Reims Cathedral.

"It is the most imposing building I have ever seen," she wrote. "It stands there towering above that ruined and desolate city like some grief-stricken mother who has lost all her children."

The letter is typical of her writing, full of images and impressions of the world she hungered to see. In 1918, after only a year on the job as director of the Norfolk Public Library, she took a leave of absence to go to Paris and serve as hostess of the YMCA there during the last months of World War I. Her job was to help soldiers and sailors with the language, customs and haunts of the city.

When she returned to Norfolk in August 1919, she told *The Virginian-Pilot*, "Naturally, I was glad to come home. But frankly, had I unlimited means at my disposal, after visiting my friends here, I'd go back to Paris, for it was the most marvelous city in the world for me."

On March 17, 2008, the City of Norfolk paid tribute to one of the outstanding women in its history when it formally opened the Mary D. Pretlow Anchor Branch of the Norfolk Public Library in Ocean View.

Pretlow's abrupt departure from the library position may have seemed impulsive to some, but not to those who knew the strong-willed woman. Mary Denson Pretlow, born on a plantation near Courtland in Southampton County in 1876, spurned the advice of relatives and

Pretlow standing at Reims
Cathedral in April 1919.
*Courtesy of the Sargeant
Memorial Room, Norfolk
Public Library.*

embarked on a career as a librarian. After graduating from the Episcopal
Female Institute in Winchester, Virginia, she trained at the New York
Public Library and, after serving as children's librarian, became manager
of a branch in one of the city's Italian neighborhoods. Later, she moved
to St. Louis and headed two of that city's library branches.

Then, in 1917, with the death of William Henry Sargeant, she became
the second director of the Norfolk Public Library. There was only the main
library in Freemason then and one branch, the Van Wyck, in Ghent. After
her return from Europe, she set a goal of opening branch libraries within
walking distance of every resident of the city. By the time she was finished
thirty years later, she had opened six of them.

It wasn't just library work that drove this determined woman. Pretlow
served on local preservation and arts groups and helped found the Little

Pretlow in a passport
photo. *Courtesy of
the Sargeant Memorial
Room, Norfolk Public
Library.*

Theater of Norfolk. Other causes had an edge. She was active in Democratic Party politics, was a member of the Women's Council for Interracial Cooperation and served as counselor for the Phyllis Wheatley Branch, the city's African American YWCA. She also succeeded in desegregating Norfolk's libraries.

There was a literary side, too. Pretlow wrote a series of articles called "Street Stories" for the *New York Evening Post,* as well as articles and criticism for several other newspapers and magazines. And even though she didn't like cooking, she managed to write two cookbooks.

She also started the Library's Sargeant Memorial Room, the extensive local history collection that recently observed its eightieth anniversary. It is the SMR that has collected numerous Pretlow papers and memorabilia, many of them from her grand-nieces. They'll be on display at the library.

She never married, but there was in her life another kind of romance. One of the most intriguing items for display is a bronze pin in the shape of a liberty figure, with a tricolor ribbon for backing. Attached is a note: "This was pinned on my lapel by a French captain July 14, 1919, in front of the Paris Opera House."

THE HUNTERS BECOME
THE HUNTED

It was six minutes after midnight on April 14, 1942, off the coast of North Carolina. Stars filled the clear night sky. With barely any wind, the sea was calm and sparkling with phosphorescence. Off the starboard side of the destroyer *Roper*, on its way south from Norfolk, the Bodie Island Light was visible.

At that moment, the radar operator saw a shape on the surface that could have been a Coast Guard vessel, but also possibly a submarine. The sound operator picked up the drone of propellers. Whatever its identity, it was a small vessel running away at high speed, frequently shifting course. The *Roper* gave chase, increasing its speed to twenty knots, and gradually drew closer.

U-boat *U-85* had left St. Nazaire, France, three weeks before on its fourth war cruise. There were about forty-five officers and men in the "iron coffin," as many called it.

On April 4, according to the diary of one of the crewmen, the sub was "just off America." On April 10, it sank a Swedish freighter, with all hands lost. On April 12, the crew spent the day lying on the bottom, waiting for nightfall. "All quiet off New York," the twenty-five-year-old seaman reported. The next morning, he observed "American beacons and searchlights visible." They were headed south, toward the Graveyard of the Atlantic.

They'd never spend another night alive.

Several minutes after the chase began, the distance between the two vessels dropped to three hundred yards. Then all doubt about the identity of the intruder vanished as a torpedo slashed by, close to the *Roper*'s port side. Suddenly, the sub turned sharply to starboard, its camouflaged side bathed in the destroyer's searchlight, and prepared to fight it out on the surface.

Machine-gun fire from the American ship kept the German crewmen from getting to their powerful 88-millimeter deck gun. A three-inch gun battery hit the conning tower at the water line and the vessel began to submerge.

"The submarine," according to the *Roper's* report, "apparently was scuttled, inasmuch as she settled slowly and went down stern first."

Scuttled or not, there were soon forty German sailors in the water, many of them crying out for help. "'Bitte [Please]! Bitte!' they were yelling. 'Kamrade. Please! Help me. Save me,'" Homer H. Hickam Jr. writes in *Torpedo Junction*.

The Americans were wary. This might have been a desperate ruse. They feared that if they stopped to rescue the survivors, the sub with its remaining crew would "move out of the killing zone and then turn back to put a torpedo into the attacking force," Hickam wrote.

The order was given to drop depth charges, set to go off at one hundred feet. The explosions instantly killed all of the men in the water.

In the morning, the *Roper* returned and removed the dead. They were taken to a hangar at Norfolk Air Station for identification, and personal effects, like the diary, were examined. Because of the secrecy of military operations, the bodies were transported at night to Hampton National Cemetery, where a detail of German prisoners was busy digging graves. A Catholic and then Protestant chaplain read burial services. A volley

Their final cruise. Graves at Hampton National Cemetery. *Courtesy of Paul Clancy.*

of three shots was fired, taps was sounded and twenty-nine young men were buried.

As you're reading this, NOAA divers are inspecting the remains of two German subs, including *U-85*, off Oregon Inlet. This "Battle of the Atlantic" project, a multiyear effort, will document the condition of the subs and some of the ships they sank in that long-ago conflict.

Along with Jeff Johnston, historian for NOAA's Monitor National Marine Sanctuary, and Shannon Ricles, education outreach coordinator, I walked among gravestones at the cemetery bordering West County Street. The sea of white markers include those of veterans of conflicts going back to the Civil War, so it's surprising to come across rows of graves that have markers indicating German seamen. Most of them give the date of death as April 14, 1942.

Typical of combatants of all countries, these were young people, somebody's son or brother, or maybe new father, snuffed out before their lives had really begun.

PLAYGROUND ON
THE CHESAPEAKE

If you grew up in this area, chances are at some point your parents rode the trolley out to Ocean View; swam in the gentle waters of the Chesapeake; rode the Skyrocket roller coaster ("the ride that thrills with perfect safety"), the Ferris wheel, the carousel and the bumper cars; bought popcorn at Hall's Texaco Station or ice cream cones at Doumar's (its original location); fished, danced and listened to concerts; and maybe necked on the last trolley back to Norfolk after the conductor obligingly dimmed the lights. Then again, perhaps you remember all of this yourself…

Ocean View, "the Atlantic City of the South," was the playground on the Chesapeake Bay that lured visitors from all over the East to its hotels and cottages, its amusement park, its casinos and nightlife. It flourished for just about a century, nearly died and then, in little more than a decade, revived again. But the old "OV" is gone—except for the memories.

Now the new Pretlow Branch of the Norfolk Public Library is open and the past is present. The library includes space for the Ocean View Station Museum, where everything Ocean View, especially the fun, honky-tonk Ocean View, is on display.

The museum, named for the trolley station that once stood at the site of the library, features, right in the center of the room, a restored roller coaster car and, nearby, a Kiddie Land boat that used to ride around a circular pond. It showcases photos, maps and other memorabilia, plus a gift counter where visitors can buy jewelry, books or poster-size photos of that place's treasured past.

And treasured it was. Although you could argue that OV's development goes all the way back to 1610, when Captain Thomas Willoughby was granted 2,900 acres along the bay front, the curtain didn't really rise until 1854. That's when a group of businessmen founded the Ocean View Company and bought

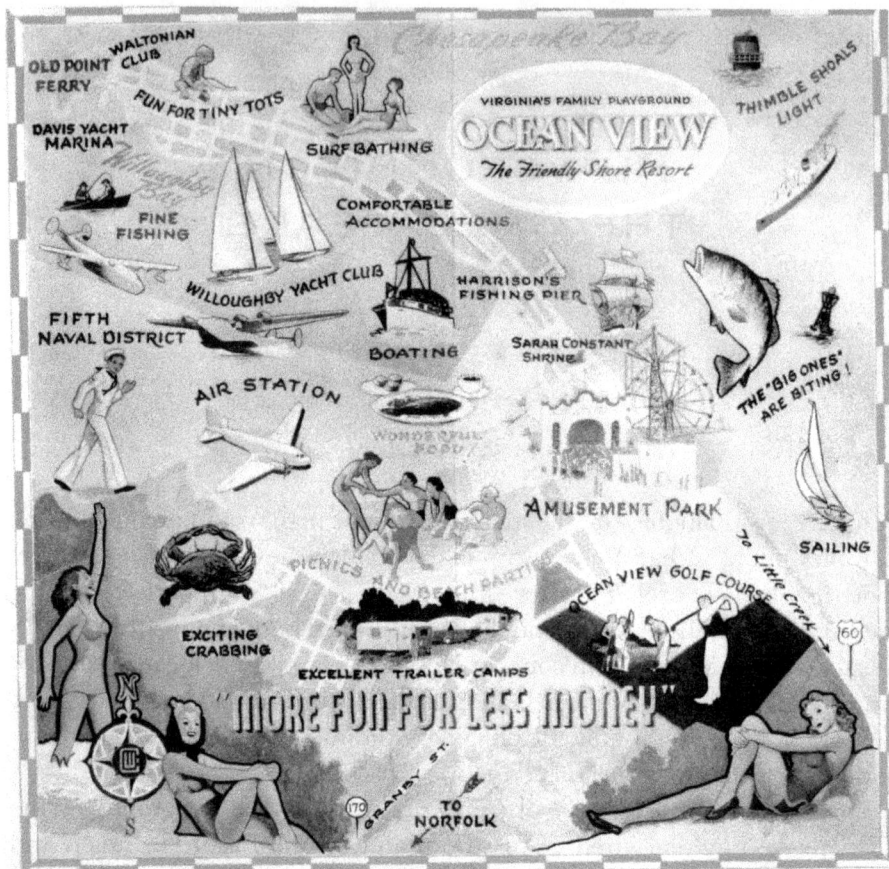

Poster of "Virginia's Family Playground." *Courtesy of Ocean View Station Museum.*

10 acres with the far-fetched notion of building a "family seaside villa." But there was nothing but a bumpy, dusty stagecoach road running out there and some bad news on the way—a massive yellow fever epidemic and, soon after, the Civil War. Its biggest claim to fame then seems to have been as the landing spot for Union troops when they captured Norfolk.

Aside from a few houses at the beach, nothing much happened until 1879 when the Ocean View Railway Co. built a narrow-gauge, single-track line that carried a tiny locomotive and three open cars to the beach. Soon, several private clubs sprang up, followed by summer cottages. The first trolleys began in Norfolk in 1891, with spurs to Sewell's Point, Ocean View and Willoughby Spit. Then came the Ocean View Amusement Park in 1899. Huge hotels like the Nansemond sprouted on the dunes alongside dozens of smaller hotels and guest cottages.

Station stop at Ocean View. *Courtesy of* The Virginian-Pilot.

Ocean View was not only a great place to vacation but also to live year round. Caroline Doonan, one of the museum's board members, has roots that go back to 1905, when her great-grandparents arrived from North Carolina and opened up a hotel called the Lowe. "They had the best food in Ocean View," she says. "I was told that when they rang the dinner bell, the sound of footsteps on the stairs was like thunder."

Her mother and father met at Florence's Drug Store, a favorite OV hangout across from the amusement park. Among her collection of photos are shots of her mother in a bathing suit vying for the title of Miss Ocean View. It was an idyllic place. "You'd get up and go to the beach every day. There were always cool breezes off the bay, and fireworks every major holiday. We could watch them from the front porch of our house."

She and I went upstairs to the library's "Kid Zone." From there, off to the west, you can see where Willoughby's mansion sat. But the view to die for is of the bay. You can see why they called it Ocean View, because you can just about see where bay and ocean blend. And you can imagine the trolley station, the hotels, dancing under the stars, cotton candy, the roar of the roller coaster, the breeze off the bay.

You're almost there.

WATCHING THE SKY ROCKET

When Joe Leatherman was eight years old, he boarded a bus in Cleveland and came to live with his father in a place called Ocean View. He was terrified for all of a few minutes. That's because his father, who worked weekends at Ocean View Amusement Park, took him straight into the park, introduced him to everyone, showed him all the rides and made him feel instantly at home in that crazy, wonderful world.

"This isn't going to be so bad," he thought.

He and his grandmother—who also worked at the park—lived in a four-room cottage a block from the park, and from his bedroom at night he could hear the magical roar of the roller coaster and the screams of its riders. If he propped his pillow just so, he could see, over the rooftop of the Rosele Theater, the Sky Rocket as it crested the first height and made its plunge.

"One more, let me see it go over one more time before I sleep," he would tell himself.

There was always music piped from the bandstand and that maniacal laugh from the mechanical lady, Laughing Sal, in the Tunnel of Fun. They filled his nights and his dreams.

Leatherman took odd jobs around the park, running change to the ticket booths and errands for the help, in exchange for tips and free rides. He hung out at the penny arcade and helped keep the pinball machines working. His first official job, at age sixteen, was manning the pooper scooper at the petting zoo.

Now fifty—with thirty years as a lineman for Cox Communications —Leatherman used his vacation to help with the installation of the new Ocean View Station Museum in the Mary Pretlow Library. The museum opened with the new branch library on March 13, 2008.

Fireworks over the roller coaster at Ocean View Amusement Park. *Courtesy of Joe Leatherman.*

Ocean View Amusement Park dates to 1899, when the Virginia Electric and Power Co. put in picnic tables at the end of the trolley line and families began to ride out to the bay's edge to swim and catch the breeze. It grew gradually and was acquired by theater impresario Otto Wells in 1928. It survived the monstrous 1933 hurricane and a blackout during World War II. Norfolk optometrist Dudley Cooper, who also owned Seaside Amusement Park in Virginia Beach, bought the park in 1942 and greatly expanded it. He also helped establish a separate Seaview Beach Amusement Park for blacks. His papers are in a special collection at Old Dominion University.

Leatherman's favorite memory is not the roller coaster but the Ferris wheel.

In the first three or four years, as it came over the top, you were facing Granby Street. It was fun. But then one year, they turned it around. So when you came around, you were looking right at the bay. I can still remember that, the first time I rode it, coming over the top. This is one of those things that takes your breath away. I used to just love that, coming over the top and just looking at all that water. I used to ask the operator…I would go get him a hamburger or Coke or something, and get a free ride. I would have him stop me at the top. When it wasn't busy, I'd just sit there until he got a rider.

At a neighborhood party, Norfolk poet Shirley Nesbit Sellers reminded me that her book, *Where the Gulls Nest*, includes a nostalgic memory of the carousel, the boardwalk and the "care-forswearing clamor" of visitors to the park. Here's part of it:

> *But the view from the ferris wheel*
> *remains a joyous lesson*
> *in leisure life*
> *and a poignant awareness*
> *of our city and its shores.*
> *Ferris wheels are found everywhere*
> *but nowhere else could one be found*
> *with a view over the bay*
> *across light-reflected waters*
> *to ships twinkling in the dark*
> *and a searchlight keeping its lonely vigil.*
> *There came to us,*
> *suspended above the world,*
> *in the dark and salty ocean breezes.*
> *a grasp of the distance and solitude*
> *a mariner knows.*

Gentlemen Preferred
Our Blonde

I came across an intriguing bit of fluff in my well-worn copy of *Norfolk, The First Four Centuries*, by Thomas C. Parramore, Peter C. Stewart and Tommy L. Bogger. It's about a Berkley girl who ran away from home at the age of fifteen and became a chorus girl and movie star. But the real claim to fame of Peggy Hopkins Joyce was how many millionaires she married and divorced—six of them. And then I found a recent book about her in the library: *Gold Digger: The Outrageous Life and Times of Peggy Hopkins Joyce*, by Constance Rosenblum. And, online, mention of an autobiography, *Men, Marriage and Me*.

As her estranged father said, when learning of her exploits, "Dern my kittens, but that is something." I'll say.

Margaret Upton grew up in the Berkley section of Norfolk, mostly with her grandparents. Her parents divorced and her father, a barber, went off to Farmville. When she was about six years old, her grandfather, "Dernie" Wood—that's the name that appears in a 1921 *Pilot* story—was shot down in the street near their home. The man who killed him claimed self-defense and got away with it.

Otherwise, Margaret had a peaceful childhood in Berkley, but she wanted something more. On one of several trips to Ocean View, she attracted the attention of one Everett Archibald, a millionaire from Denver, who asked her for a dance and was apparently smitten by her. After several meetings in Atlantic City, they were married, but a quick annulment followed and she was on her way to way to fortune, if not yet fame. She married Sherburne Hopkins, son of a prominent lawyer, in Washington, D.C., but left him almost before the marriage papers were signed.

It was then off to New York, where "Peggy" starred in a Ziegfeld Follies review, *Miss 1918*. On a road show in Chicago, she met and married lumber king J. Stanley Joyce. "Peggy locked herself in a bathroom on her wedding night and refused to come out until he slid a check for $500,000 under the door," the Norfolk historians write. "She was soon off to Paris and later took Joyce for $2 million in a divorce settlement." At about this time, the dazzling blonde was spotted by W.C. Fields, the bigger-than-life character actor, who taught her to say her first stage lines. She moved on to leading roles on Broadway and a half dozen or so movies.

But she grew bored with movies, especially the hard work of early morning studio calls, preferring instead her life as a socialite and the center of attention. Among those who showered her with attention and diamond necklaces were Averell Harriman, Hiram Bloomingdale, Prince Christopher of Greece and Walter Chrysler. There were three other marriages and, she claimed in her own book, at least fifty engagements. An AP story said she emerged from all these encounters "with substantial bank accounts and jewelry filled deposit boxes." One Website, www.filmsofthegoldenage.com, says she was the inspiration for the film *Gentlemen Prefer Blonds*.

"I may be expensive," she was once quoted as saying, "but I deliver the goods."

She died of throat cancer in 1957 at age sixty-two. This is approximate because she always declined to reveal her age.

It's hard to say whether she was terribly happy about her life. Constance Rosenblum, the biographer, said she wasn't especially talented or smart but was nonetheless oddly likeable. "She knew what she wanted, went for it with her whole heart, and lived the life she yearned to live."

WHERE DO WE GO FROM HERE?

A ll that remains is the bell tower and one of the brick walls. Red doors, with windows in the shape of crosses, once opened into the vestibule of the church but now lead to a massive pile of rubble. Gone are the elaborately painted ceiling, gone the towering stained-glass windows, the antique pulpit, the communion table, the baptismal pool.

Portsmouth's venerable Zion Baptist Church—the building at least—is no more. But what couldn't be destroyed is the history of a church that was born during one of the nation's climactic moments and served its people for generations.

Part of the church's story can be found in brochures that were produced for its centennial celebration in 1965; part, also, in records and books in the Local History Room of the Portsmouth Public Library; and part in the memories of its members.

The "mother church" of Zion Baptist, as its own literature calls it, was the white-owned Court Street Baptist Church. Before the Civil War, blacks and whites in the region worshipped together, although it was always clear that churches were run by whites. In fact, before the war, Virginia passed a law forbidding black persons, whether slave or free, from gathering to listen to their own preachers. In Portsmouth, which spent much of the war under Union occupation, tensions ran high among whites whose sons fought for the South and blacks who joined "colored" units and fought for the North.

Then there's this: the hated Union general Benjamin F. Butler had the Court Street Church's minister imprisoned and its building taken over as a hospital for Northern troops. By war's end, it was time for a parting of the ways. At their request, the church allowed 318 blacks to give up their memberships and form their own congregation. It was March 9, 1865, the official beginning of Zion Baptist Church.

All that remained of historic Zion Baptist Church in Portsmouth. *Photo by Steve Earley, courtesy of* The Virginian-Pilot.

It was apparently an amicable parting because the congregation met for the first year in the Court Street Church basement. The location it settled on was at King and Green Streets, and the property was the first owned by African Americans in the city's history. One of the breakaway church members, E.G. Corprew, a self-taught man who amassed a considerable library, was ordained its first minister.

The first church, a wooden structure, lasted only from 1866 to 1869, when a fire burned it to the ground. The members met in a firehouse at the corner of High and Washington Streets until a new church, this time of brick, could be finished in 1876. A second brick church, the most recent, dated to 1894.

In its 140 years, Zion Baptist Church played major roles in the city's history and its community life, establishing missions throughout town to help feed, clothe and educate the underprivileged. Among its most prominent ministers was the Reverend John M. Armistead, one of the great pulpit orators of his day who, during the 1880s, served on Portsmouth City Council. Seventy or so years later, the Reverend Horace Edward Whitaker was a friend of the Reverend Martin Luther King Jr. at Crozier Theological Seminary in Chester, Pennsylvania. Among King's papers is a 1954 letter in which he closes, "Well, ole' timer, whatever you do, continue to 'preach the word,' in season and out of season." It's addressed to "Mike," King's name then, and signed "Whit."

Across Green Street from the burned-out building is the H. Edward Whitaker Educational Building. It's all that's left of the church complex. From inside, where volunteers meet to carry on church programs, you would not know that Zion Baptist had suffered a devastating loss just a month before. The church still runs a large homeless program and organizes several of its other neighborhood ministries there.

Mary Todd, a member of the church for sixty-five years, said her reaction to the fire was to remember all the children she has taught in Sunday school and Bible classes who have now come back with children of their own. "It's more than just a building to me, it's more than just furniture," she said. "It's memories."

The church now meets in an auditorium at the Sheriff's Academy at Randolph and Green Streets. One Wednesday, the Reverend Thomas T. Shields was working on his sermon for Sunday morning. He planned to use as text the title of Dr. King's book, "Where Do We Go From Here?" and a passage from Proverbs about acknowledging God and letting Him show the way. At this point in the church's long history, he said, God is clearly saying, "'I don't want you to build a church building. I want you to build ministries.'"

Shields displayed the only things saved from the fire: more than a dozen brass collection plates, a few blackened, but others only slightly tarnished, with felt bottoms still intact. "This is all we need," he said.

POOR LITTLE PEPPINA

One of the amazing things about history is that you can get lost in it. Hopelessly lost.

I had thought this time I'd take a look back at the Granby Theater, the once-grand movie palace that reopened as a nightclub and concert venue a couple of years ago but now seems threatened. I stopped at the Sargeant Memorial Room of the Kirn Library and read through a file of newspaper clippings that helped set the scene. It was February 21, 1916, when the "most complete and most up-to-date strictly motion picture theater in the South" opened, reported *The Virginian-Pilot*. More than six thousand people paid ten cents each to crowd into the spacious theater over the course of an afternoon and evening. At one point the crowd outside spilled into the street and blocked traffic, requiring the local constabulary to restore order.

All the fuss was over a film in which "America's Sweetheart," Mary Pickford, stars as *Poor Little Peppina*, a waif who is kidnapped by a Mafioso and whisked off to Italy. Years later, the pretty mop-haired girl escapes the clutches of a cruel padrone, stows away and flees to America. Hardships there—the same mobster, for one—are finessed with the help of a rich admirer she encountered on the ship.

Sidetracked, I looked up everything I could about Pickford, the former Gladys Smith from Toronto, who more or less created the movie megastar. I rented a documentary about her at Naro Expanded Video and was lost in details of her love affair with, then marriage to, Douglas Fairbanks. Oh, and by the way, the dashing Fairbanks was starring in a film at the Wells Theater, *His Picture in the Paper*, at the same time that Pickford's offering graced the Granby.

Curiosity about the theater led me to reel through microfilm for other events of that day, and I was sucked deeper into the quicksand of history.

A parade, probably mid-1950s, passes by the Granby Theater. *Courtesy of the Granby Theater.*

Among other things, it was a day that Anti-Saloon League forces in Richmond—they were all over the country at the time, a huge, powerful organization—pushed the state senate closer to prohibition. A constitutional amendment banning the sale of alcoholic beverages was now only a couple of years off.

At the same time in Norfolk, a score of preachers met at Cumberland Street Methodist Church to push for a law banning red-light districts. They vowed to do all they could "to rescue the fallen ones and to purify the community." Thank goodness.

Similarly, a group of Baptists lamented about "the vice situation in Norfolk and Portsmouth." If that weren't enough news of the day, at about the same time that *Poor Little Peppina* was flickering on the screen at the Granby, the earth shook.

The newspaper reported on the front page,

There was a slight earthquake in Norfolk yesterday evening about 6:40 o'clock. There is no official record of the quake because there is no seismograph here to record earth shocks. The weather bureau reports, however, that from the best information obtainable there was a slight tremor of the earth noticeable in this city. It lasted about ten seconds and appeared to be moving in an easterly direction.

That day there was also a remarkable photo, taken by a crew member of a Coast Guard cutter, of a coal-laden barge taking on water and sinking. The barge had left Norfolk under tow, bound for New England, when it apparently ran into heavy seas and sank in Lynnhaven Bay.

Hanging over all the paper's coverage was an event far more ominous than sinking barges, teetotalling senators, pious preachers and, certainly, silent screen stars. It was the monster that had been uncaged in Europe. At the time that film reels were whirring in the theater, French and German forces were attacking and counterattacking each other at a place called Verdun. The French held, but at a sickening cost of lives. President Wilson was attempting peace overtures, but within a year the United States would be drawn into the death trap.

There's a World War I echo in Norfolk streets. Driving out Lafayette Avenue, you see the names: Somme, Vimy Ridge, Argonne, Verdun, Marne…All battles on distant soil. But that's another story.

Now, let's see, where was I going with this…?

WATERSIDE AND
THE MAN WHO MADE
CITIES FUN AGAIN

O n the original 1680 plan for "Norfolk Town," recreated by Rogers Dey Whichard, there's a road that cuts through the middle of town. It's labeled "The Roadway That Leadeth to the Waterside." It ends almost exactly where, about three centuries later, urban visionary James W. Rouse decided that the renaissance of the city's downtown should begin. "The Waterside," he originally called it. In June 1983, a place bearing that name opened with great fanfare and promise.

A parade of numerous bands and an assortment of clowns, jugglers, mimes, belly dancers and antique cars snaked through downtown and then streamed by the gleaming glass-and-steel structure on the waterfront. A navy band swung into "Anchors Aweigh." Lynda Robb, wife of the governor, cracked a confetti-filled champagne bottle against a railing. A couple of dozen tugboats standing off in the harbor released a cloud of red, white and blue balloons into a misty rain. And an enthusiastic crowd descended on the brand-new marketplace to sample the fare at 122 restaurants, markets, specialty shops, kiosks and pushcarts.

"With the great spirit of the people here and the beauty of the Waterside," Rouse declared the night before, "I think we're about to embark on something that will be a smashing success."

The nice part of this story, unlike other dashed urban schemes, is that Waterside did exactly what it was supposed to do. It became a magnet for tourists, shoppers and investors that led to what has been called an urban miracle. There's no doubt that it fulfilled the dream of the man who envisioned it.

Ironically, Rouse had helped accelerate the decline of cities by building, before anyone else, enclosed shopping malls in suburban areas. But he later came to deplore the "mindlessness" of suburban sprawl and clutter and launched, almost simultaneously, two major counterattacks.

James Rouse in front of the newly opened Waterside. *Courtesy of* The Virginian-Pilot.

One was the new town of Columbia, Maryland, on fourteen thousand acres of farmland between Washington and Baltimore. It was organized around eight villages, each with its own shopping center and elementary school. The villages were interconnected not only with roadways but with walking and biking trails as well. There was a mix of housing for different income levels and lifestyles, recreational facilities and open space. It introduced the novel idea that people didn't need to get in a car every time they went somewhere. The "new town" concept, to one extent or another, caught on across America.

Then Rouse did something equally radical. He decided to help rescue declining cities by building "festival marketplaces" that would bring people back downtown. These places—Faneuil Hall in Boston, Harborplace in Baltimore, South Street Seaport in New York and Union Station in St. Louis—were enormously successful. As *Time Magazine* said in a cover story, he was "the man who made cities fun again."

He'd been to Norfolk on a couple of earlier occasions. It was on one of these forays that he met his second wife, Patricia Traugott, who was then a member of the Norfolk Redevelopment and Housing Authority. There would be numerous roadblocks in his vision for Norfolk but he wasn't the sort to take no for an answer.

"He called me one day and said he wanted to go look at the waterfront for a place to build a festival marketplace," said Harvey Lindsay, a commercial realtor, swiveling around to look across to Waterside from his fourteenth-floor Dominion Tower office. "I'll never forget it. We started in Freemason and stopped right there. 'This is where it should be,' he said."

Waterside was completely leased out, with only one thing missing: Lindsay remembers Rouse scolding him for not finding an old-fashioned butcher. That's how fussy Rouse was about selecting just the right mix for these marketplaces.

One of the most fascinating things about Rouse was that he not only tried to rescue cities, but he also attempted to rescue people from the squalor of substandard housing. With the profits from his urban investments, he formed the Enterprise Foundation and, using tax incentives, public and private grants, donated materials and volunteers, helped build thousands of homes in dozens of cities. Patricia Rouse still serves on the board of what is now Enterprise Community Partners.

"He was one of the finest human spirits I've ever known," Lindsay said. "He was dedicated to helping the underprivileged and the poor. He just felt if they could get decent housing, the rest would follow."

Twenty-five years after its founding, it looks as though the engine that drove the redevelopment of downtown needs some new sparkplugs. Maybe a new vision. Or visionary.

SHE PUT HER CAREER
ON THE LINE

It's hard to imagine the courage it must have taken. She was a high school teacher in the segregated South being asked to risk her job by standing up against a system that, no matter how unfair, was deeply ingrained in her hometown. She must have known the consequences.

And yet, Aline Elizabeth Black was acutely aware of the disparity between white and black schoolteacher salaries. She had been teaching chemistry at Booker T. Washington High for twelve years and held a master's degree from the University of Pennsylvania. But she received about two-thirds the salary of her similarly educated white counterparts. The same was true for all black teachers in the system who were, in fact, paid less than white janitors in their schools.

Today, it seems like simple fairness. But this was 1938, before civil rights laws were on the books. The only guarantee of equal treatment resided in vague guarantees of equal protection of the laws and due process in the U.S. Constitution. That is, if someone could convince a judge or two, and, ultimately, the Supreme Court. Meanwhile, what about her job? What about her community? If she couldn't work here, where would she go?

But someone had to take the first step, and she agreed. In October 1938, Black petitioned the Norfolk School Board to "adopt and enforce a new salary schedule equal as to all teachers and principals with the same qualifications and experience and without any distinction being made as to race or color."

It was a wrenching time for her. Celestyne Diggs Porter, a ninety-six-year-old fellow teacher at Booker T. Washington, says she was an excellent teacher. "I saw her goodness. She was a lovely person."

The city did not deny the facts of her case but contended that she waived her rights to seek redress when she willingly signed her yearly contract. Her attorneys countered that this might be true, but that didn't give the school board the right to violate her constitutional rights. Still, her petition was denied and she went to court. Standing at her side was a young man about her age, thirty-year-old NAACP chief counsel Thurgood Marshall, who would go on to win almost every major civil rights lawsuit in America and become the first black justice of the Supreme Court. But even Marshall knew that this case, at that time, would be difficult and that Black's job would be in jeopardy.

The following spring, the school board voted unanimously not to renew her contract. *The Virginian-Pilot* denounced the board's action, calling it "an act of reprisal in which it can take no pride." In a final slap, the school board deducted $4.01 from her last paycheck because of the time she had taken off to go to court.

The civil rights movement in America barely existed, although, according to Norfolk State University historian Tommy Bogger, blacks in Norfolk had regularly observed Emancipation Day with marches and speeches throughout the city. But these were celebrations, not protests. On Sunday, June 24, 1939, black students, accompanied by a Boy Scout drum and bugle corps, marched through town, some carrying signs proclaiming "School Board Must Go" and denouncing "Dictators." Later, a crowd of about 1,200, including a few whites, gathered at St. John's AME Church to add their protest.

Black was forced to look elsewhere for a job. She went to New York and began work on a doctorate at New York University—although she grew discouraged, she said at the time, because she doubted it would land her a job.

It sounds like a Catch-22, but the NAACP dropped her case because she was no longer working for the school system. Instead, Melvin O. Alston, president of the Norfolk Teachers Association, was chosen to continue the suit. In February 1940, a state court again dismissed the case, but a federal appeals court held that the salary disparity was discriminatory and instructed the school board to adjust the salaries. The board appealed to the U.S. Supreme Court and lost. Eventually, the city agreed to phase in the increases over a three-year period. It was not what Marshall had hoped for, but it was a victory for teachers throughout the state and the South.

In 1941, Black was rehired by the Norfolk School Board and returned to teaching. She retired in 1973 and died one year later.

Black's place in local history stems from the courage she was able to muster. Says historian Bogger, "She put everything on the line."

A NEW YEAR OF HOPE

In late 1958, on New Year's Eve or a day before, a courtly man with a thin mustache rolled a page into his typewriter and, perhaps gazing out the window for a moment at ships in the harbor, adjusted his half-frame glasses and began writing. "So far as the future histories of this state can be anticipated now," he wrote, "the year 1958 will be best known as the year Virginia closed the public schools."

Lenoir Chambers, editor of *The Virginian-Pilot*, was warming to the task. It was he and he alone of the major newspapers in the state who took a stand against the state's policies of massive resistance and, in particular, the closing of public schools to avoid desegregating them. No community in Virginia suffered more than Norfolk, denying public education to thousands of students and receiving a black eye in the process.

Norfolk was caught in the vise of state law, an act by the legislature to close any school that was forced by federal courts to desegregate. On September 28, 1958, when the city attempted to carry out the court order, Governor J. Lindsay Almond Jr. ordered the doors at Granby, Maury and Norview High Schools and Blair, Northside and Norview Junior Highs chained and padlocked.

Chambers, a sixty-seven-year-old southerner and author of a two-volume biography of Stonewall Jackson, was appalled. "The punishment of innocent children is too severe," he wrote. "The desertion of a doctrine of education on which democracy itself rests runs too much against basic American convictions and beliefs, many of which first originated or first found nobility of expression in Virginia."

In shutting down public education on which democracy rests, he wrote, we were "condemning ourselves to darkness." Again and again, in clear, unwavering, logical prose—as former managing editor Robert Mason put it—he guided the community through the crisis.

Lenoir Chambers, editor of *The Virginian-Pilot*, who won the Pulitzer Prize for his editorials against massive resistance. *Courtesy of* The Virginian-Pilot.

For his work throughout the year that followed, Chambers received the Pulitzer Prize for excellence in editorial writing. Fittingly, it was the editor he succeeded, Louis Jaffe, who had won the newspaper's first Pulitzer for his passionate support of black causes, particularly his 1928 denunciation of lynching as "an unspeakable act of savagery."

Chambers was born in Charlotte. His personal reference file, preserved in crumbling envelopes in the newspaper's news library, shows that his father made cotton ginning machinery, steam engines and sawmills. After graduating from the University of North Carolina, he taught school for a couple of years, studied journalism at Columbia University and then joined the army and fought in the trenches of France and Germany during World War I. He could not have known this, but the man who would be his boss and mentor, Jaffe, had done the same thing, going off to fight in that terrible war.

When Chambers returned, he began a long and distinguished career in newspapers, beginning as a reporter at the *Greensboro Daily News*. He came to Norfolk in 1929, working as associate editor and then editor of the *Ledger-Dispatch*. On Jaffe's death in 1950, he took over as editor of the *Pilot*.

He was an imposing figure, portraits of him say, although he was hard to see behind the newspapers, magazines and books piled on his desk. He'd have to stand, in tweed suit and carelessly tied striped tie, to conduct daily editorial conferences with his associates. No one knew what the top of that desk looked like. Chambers was widely read and his editorials were laced with intelligence. He was as comfortable writing about foreign affairs as regional ones.

But it was his leadership through Norfolk's dark hours for which Chambers will be remembered. On New Year's Eve 1959, after schools had reopened, he wrote optimistically about the future. "If Virginia can produce more willingness to face the facts and fresh qualities of initiation and leadership in dealing with them, the year the state opened the schools can lead to a New Year of Hope."

AN ART BONANZA

In July 1969, Norfolk mayor Roy Martin got a call from a former classmate at Maury High School. They had one of the most important phone conversations in the city's history.

The story goes back to 1908, when Walter P. Chrysler Sr. saw his first automobile at an exposition in Chicago. His fascination became an obsession that led him to produce his own car and amass one of the greatest fortunes in the world. And it led his son, Walter Jr., to ponder what he would do with all the money he would inherit.

This is one of several fascinating parts of a book by Peggy Earle, *Legacy, Walter Chrysler Jr. and the Untold Story of Norfolk's Chrysler Museum of Art*. Earle is a former book review editor for *The Virginian-Pilot*. It's the story of the transformation of a modest provincial museum to one of America's best, thanks to an eccentric and driven man who devoted his life and fortune to collecting works of art and, finally, giving them away.

Jean Esther Outland, daughter of Lida Maddox and Grover Cleveland Outland of South Norfolk, "was cheerful and lively," Earle writes, someone "who could light up a room. She was always ready for a party—and especially an opportunity to dance." And by most accounts it was at a dance in 1944 that she met her future husband.

As chance would have it, Walter Chrysler had volunteered for the navy in 1942. But he was not your average sailor: thirty-two years old and already a world traveler, Broadway and Hollywood producer and, oh yes, one of America's most impressive art collectors.

He was not your average sailor in other ways. A 1955 *Confidential Magazine* article entitled "The Strange Case of Walter Chrysler Jr." reported that he was forced to resign by the secretary of the navy because of "notorious wild parties" at his home in Key West. Another report,

Walter met his future wife, Jean Outland, when he was in the navy in Norfolk. *Courtesy of Chrysler Museum of Art.*

according to Earle, has Chrysler being discharged because he was "found to be gay."

Walter and Jean were married in a simple ceremony at Freemason Baptist Church in January 1945. They lived in a fabulous Park Avenue apartment and mansion in Northern Virginia while at the same time he continued his obsession with collecting art. As the collection grew, he sought more space and settled on a one-time church in Provincetown, Massachusetts, then an artists' and writers' enclave.

But the collection was soon bursting at the seams, and its owner let it be known that he was looking for a major museum to house it. He received 147 applications from around the country and considered 50 of them, including museums in Denver, Houston and Oakland. But it was the Italianate Norfolk Museum of Arts and Science that most intrigued him.

Earle doesn't speculate how far Mayor Martin's jaw dropped when Jean Chrysler called him, but it's clear he saw it as a possible cultural bonanza for the city. "Without hesitation I said of course we were interested," he wrote in a memoir.

Chrysler's one stipulation was that the museum change its name, and not every city leader was thrilled with this. Some even fought against the proposal. But the city agreed, even throwing in the naming rights for the new symphony hall. Earle sets the scene for the deal-making in the office of City Manager Thomas Maxwell, as told by banker Jack Gibson.

"And Roy [the mayor] came out while I was explaining to the bigwigs of Norfolk, saying, 'Now we gotta sell this guy!' Roy says, 'Jack! Shut up!' At which point, Maxwell came out of his office with his arm around Chrysler. 'And the damn deal is done,' said Gibson. 'It is done!'"

And so it was.

A SMALL TOWN BECOMES
HOME TO FIGHTER JETS

In 1883, when train service began from Norfolk to Virginia Beach, the next-to-last stop before the oceanfront was a crossroads village called Tunis. This sudden boon for the little berg caught the attention of investors, who bought up two hundred acres in an area known as Salisbury Plain—not to be confused with the great plateau in central England where Stonehenge rests. This was the flat, flat farmland of east central Princess Anne County. When the residents sought to incorporate, they discovered that there already was a Tunis, Virginia, way out in the mountains, so they hit upon a marvelous sounding name for a place close to the beachfront, Oceana.

And the place took off, becoming one of the most populous towns in the county. The community, centered approximately where Virginia Beach Boulevard meets First Colonial Road, included a fire station, post office, grocery, gas stations and all the other ingredients of a small town. And on streets like Michigan, Indiana and Ohio and lanes like Louisa, West and Middle were hunkered several blocks of modest bungalows, Cape Cods, Arts and Crafts homes and Sears kit houses. Eastern Shore Chapel, which would eventually be moved over to Hilltop, and Scott Memorial United Methodist Church—circa 1872—were where many of the good folks went on Sundays.

According to Stephen Mansfield, author of *Princess Anne County and Virginia Beach: A Pictorial History*, a family named Potter sold 328 nearby acres to the navy for an airfield in 1940. They were all prop planes then, and there wasn't a problem with decibels. Then, at about the time Virginia Beach became a city in 1963, jets were screaming off runways. Meanwhile, other neighborhoods sprang up nearby and Oceana began losing its identity as Oceana Naval Air Station swallowed the name. It is fair to say that few living in Virginia Beach today know there was such a place, except for residents who have long lived there.

Sam Reid, president of Oceana Civic Association. *Photo by Delores Johnson, courtesy of* The Virginian-Pilot.

Recently, I met Sam Reid, president of the Oceana Civic Association and, as much as anyone, "mayor" of the village. Reid, age fifty-one, grew up in Oceana, spent twenty years as a navy sonar tech and now works as a carpenter for the school system. We sat in the yard of his 1915 home on Middle Lane near a magnificent magnolia tree. As we talked, FA-18 Hornets did touch-and-go exercises at the airfield. The runway seems to point right at the heart of the village and the jets thunder so loud you have to take what Reid calls "Oceana beer breaks"—that is, you pause long enough for a couple of sips—and then resume your conversation. If you're having a beer, of course.

His father-in-law, Dalton "Chick" Midgett, who has lived at Oceana since 1943, ambled over from next door, and the two men told me everything I wanted to know about the village. And more.

The best-known store in the little downtown was McKinney's Grocery, with large floor planks and a potbelly stove. Next to it was Ben Frank's Hotdogs, where a cutout of Benjamin Franklin could be seen flying his kite. Now that corner of First Colonial is occupied by a Wawa. Across the street, where there's now a car lot, was a popular farmers' market that sold just about everything. In the 1950s and '60s, there was a wild west show, "with a corral and all that stuff," Reid said. "Like a regular town, it had all the amenities."

And like a regular town, the neighbors all know one another. "It's like a time capsule of the 1950s, here in this neighborhood," Reid said.

We went for a drive through the village. "There's Louise Luxford's home," he'd say. She was a teacher for whom an elementary school was named. Then: "The fire chief, Jim Ed Moore, lived in that brick house." Out on the boulevard, he pointed to the former site of the farmers' market. "That's where Dad always got watermelon. You knew they were right off the farm." "That's where a guy used to hang a honey-for-sale sign." "That's where there used to be an ESSO station."

But even as Virginia Beach and the navy seek to reduce residential development in the path of the jets, growth pressures continue. The civic association wants the city to grant Oceana historical district status, making it harder for developers to tear down older houses and stopping commercial encroachment in the neighborhood.

"It used to be a little town," he said. "But it's getting more and more like Independence Boulevard."

BONE IN HER TEETH

This is a story that goes back more than two hundred years to when the great ports of Norfolk and Baltimore were engaged in a fierce maritime rivalry, with the fastest ships getting the best prices for oysters, peanuts and other money commodities. The competition inspired the construction of strong, sleek schooners that were works of pure grace and speed.

That contest reached a new level at 00:58 on October 12, 2007, when the schooner *Virginia*, with Maryland's *Pride of Baltimore II* close astern, took first place in the Great Chesapeake Bay Schooner Race, smashing the course record by more than an hour.

The modern rivalry began in 1990 when Lane Briggs, captain of the odd but loveable schooner-rigged tug *Norfolk Rebel* challenged the skipper of the *Pride* to a down-the-bay race, with the prize being a beer or two at a bar of the winner's choice. The race, now benefiting the Chesapeake Bay Foundation, evolved into a major event, with forty or more of the tall ships battling each other every October for something a little more valuable than suds: bragging rights. Briggs, until he died two years ago, watched over the fleet like a mother hen, going to the aid of anyone needing assistance.

The *Pride*, a replica of an 1812-era clipper privateer, was always a force to be reckoned with. Low slung and carrying far more sail than anyone else, the pride of Maryland as well as Baltimore came in first in its class year after year. If only they could beat the *Pride*, designers and skippers of other sailing vessels lamented.

In fact, other, more modern, schooners began winning in recent years. The lightning-fast *Imagine...!* out of Annapolis crossed the line at Thimble Shoals off Hampton in 2005 with a seemingly impossible elapsed time of twelve hours, fifty-seven minutes. Surely, that record would never be broken.

Neck-and-neck race between the schooner *Virginia*, in the lead, and the *Pride of Baltimore II* in the Great Chesapeake Schooner Race, October 2007. *Courtesy of the Virginia Maritime Heritage Foundation.*

But from the start, when the *Virginia* was still on the drawing boards as the state's world-roving goodwill ambassador, the 119-foot boat's designers dared to dream.

They took their design from a 1917 pilot schooner that happened to be named *Virginia*. Built and owned by the Virginia Pilot Association to train future pilots, the ship was built for hustle. Legend has it that the *Virginia* once raced from Cape Henry to Old Point Comfort at average speeds in excess of fifteen knots. Under certain conditions, the new *Virginia*, built like a champion of the best South American hardwoods, might someday do very well in a flat-out race.

At the start off in Annapolis on Thursday, October 11, 2007, both the *Virginia* and the *Pride* went for speed across the line, swiftly blowing past the other racers as fifteen- to twenty-knot northwesterly winds, gusting almost to thirty, shoved them along. The *Virginia*, which does well in such conditions, quickly took the lead, although not by much.

Jonathan Gorog, executive director of the Virginia Maritime Heritage Foundation, builder of the *Virginia* and a member of the guest crew, said the sight of the *Pride*'s impressive sails lit by the setting sun was "a magical and beautiful sight." After dark, all they saw was the red or green navigation lights as their rival jockeyed for a chance to overtake them. "With the *Pride* breathing down our neck, it was a waste of time to go below even for a minute."

"The boat was flying, with all sails set and a bone in her teeth," the *Virginia*'s captain, Nicholas Alley, writes in the ship's blog. "Looking aft, the sight of *Pride II* was scary, all that sail, the spray from her bow wave, and all headed for us! This screaming ride continued into the night, with *Pride II* right on our stern, looking for the opportunity to catch us." At one point, Alley told me, the boat reached fourteen knots.

When the wind moved to the north, which was more favorable to the *Pride*, the distance between the two closed to less than a mile. But this changed as another, more westerly, shift allowed the *Virginia* to ease ahead and cross the finish line with an unheard-of elapsed time of eleven hours, eighteen minutes, with Maryland's champion a blink of an eye, nine minutes, behind.

Hardly anyone slept a wink.

SNAKE CREEK AND
YAUPON TEA

"We're floating through history," she says as we cruise south on the North Landing River. "This liquid highway is more than a way to get somewhere; it's a way to jump into the past."

Lillie Gilbert, avid outdoorswoman and keen historian, is at it again with her naturalist sidekick, Vickie Shufer. They're setting out once again to paddle their way through Virginia Beach's little-known waterways. It's a windy day in late March, and they're about to explore a couple of the only creeks in the region that have not felt the blade of their paddles.

The two authors meet Bill Spaur, a retired navy physician, and his friend Ruth Bizot at the old Pungo Marina on the North Landing River. With Barb and I joining them, the plan is for Spaur to tow our canoes downriver with his sturdy twenty-five-foot powerboat, *Grace*, to the suspected entrances to Snake and Walnut Creeks (Virginia Beach maps don't name them but NOAA charts do). From there, we'll investigate the waterways.

Gilbert and Shufer are two of the most enthusiastic canoeists-kayakers in our part of the world. They have written three guidebooks for paddlers, naturalists and historians on local waterways. The most recent includes just about every stretch of water from Corolla, North Carolina, to Cape Henry. Now they're updating the first, *Wild River Guide to the North Landing and its Tributaries*.

The North Landing, then called "North River," was first mentioned in a 1672 map of Carolina. It is best known today by boaters as part of the Intracoastal Waterway that flows inland all the way to Florida. It connects to the Elizabeth River by way of a canal through Great Bridge. Therein lies one of the little-known turning points of local history.

There were proposals during the colonial era to dig the canal not through Great Bridge but through Kemp's Landing, a one-time burgeoning village.

Vickie Shufer, at the bow, and Lillie Gilbert, at the stern, exploring one of the creeks off the North Landing River in Virginia Beach. *Courtesy of Paul Clancy.*

The canal would have linked North Carolina and Norfolk by way of the eastern branch of the Elizabeth, rather than the southern branch, and perhaps establish the future Kempsville as a major Virginia Beach seaport. The other route was chosen, however, because it was slightly shorter. Kempsville's star was eclipsed.

A reminder of the once-prosperous trade route is still visible on the North Landing. As we motor past Munden Point Park, Gilbert points to remnants of piers where steamboats offloaded produce for transport by rail to Norfolk. She shows us a 1905 map that includes the "Norfolk, Virginia Beach & Southern R.R., Currituck Division," with stops that included Princess Anne Courthouse, Pungo, Back Bay, Creeds and Munden Point. The trade that poured through this water conduit was prodigious.

We anchor near duck blinds just off the entrances to Snake and Walnut Creeks and transfer to the canoes. There is no history to be explored here, except the recent history of redwing blackbird nests and, in trees off in the distance, last year's eagle nests. We paddle along corridors of tall cord grass and examine what Shufer identifies as blue-flag iris, bog cranberry and an otter lodge. We marvel at a flock of black wing–tipped snow geese and shudder at the shadow of a turkey vulture passing overhead.

Later, heading back to Pungo Ferry, Gilbert shows me a copy of Nathaniel Bishop's classic 1878 book, *Voyage of the Paper Canoe*. It relates the explorer's journey from Quebec to the Gulf of Mexico in a light, resin-soaked paper vessel through these waters. At one of his stops, the Pungo Ferry operator, a one-time slave, puts him up for the night. An "ancient dame" stops by to light her short-stemmed pipe and discourse on the virtues of yaupon tea. "You can't reckon how I longs to get a cup of good yaupon," she soliloquizes.

And then the freedman, content in his Pungo shanty, ends his own story with: "O that was a glorious day for me/When Massa Lincoln set me free."

ON THE SHOULDERS
OF MANY

The victory of President Barack Obama resonates through Virginia history like distant thunder.

It was here, late one summer day in 1619, when, sailing out of a violent storm, a Dutch warship made port at Old Point Comfort. In its cargo hold were twenty or so Africans who had been stolen from a Portuguese ship. Being short of food, the captain and crew traded their human cargo for provisions and sailed off. The new arrivals were treated, at first, as indentured servants. But as the tobacco economy continued to demand cheap labor, the screws began to tighten, and within a couple of decades, thousands of imported Africans were bought and sold as slaves. So it is not a stretch to observe that the institution of slavery and the sorrowful centuries that followed originated in Hampton Roads. It would take more than two hundred years, and finally a civil war, to put an end to slavery, and then another century to begin erasing the system of segregation that followed.

There was a poignant reminder in the South Hill section of Chesapeake a few days after the election. In a small park on Bannister Street, the Chesapeake Parks and Recreation Department and the Bells Mill Historic Research and Restoration Society unveiled a plaque marking the spot where the South Hill Colored School once stood. Like thousands of similar schools throughout the South, this four-room schoolhouse offered an earnestly provided, but inherently unequal, education to generations of students.

The school, which opened in 1921 and closed in 1964, had four classrooms and an office. There was no central heating, unless you count a potbelly stove, and no flushing toilets for about 140 students and four teachers. It was built by the Norfolk County Board of Education, with help from the Julius Rosenwald Fund and the Colored Community School League. Rosenwald, then president of Sears, Roebuck and Co.,

South Hill Colored School, a four-room building that opened in 1921 in South Norfolk, now part of Chesapeake. *Courtesy of E. Curtis Alexander.*

helped build more than five thousand schools, stores and teachers' homes throughout the South. The Colored Community School League raised the matching funds for the schoolhouse.

Segregated schools were supposedly "separate but equal," but they weren't. "We got the worst of everything," said E. Curtis Alexander, a prominent Chesapeake historian, who attended nearby Bells Mill Colored School. "We got second- and third-hand books—and in the early days no books at all. The school days were shorter. The school year was shorter. Teachers were paid less. In 1942, my homeroom teacher, James Riddick, filed a suit for equal pay on behalf of the Norfolk County Teachers' Association."

Public officials were there at the plaque unveiling, including Mayor Alan Krasnoff, members of city council and the Chesapeake School Board, but the most important attendees were twenty-two former students of the South Hill School. They posed for pictures beside the sign as late morning sun broke over the small park where the school once stood.

Among them was Mary Butler, born in 1920, who began school there at age six. "My momma's home was right over there," she said, pointing to land now occupied by Interstate 464. "I can remember all my teachers. I thank God for letting me be here all these eighty-eight years."

Her daughter, Sheila Vines, also went to the school, leaving in 1964, the year the schools began to desegregate. At the time, she said, she and her classmates weren't aware—not then—of discrimination. "Everybody was a family," she said.

Lacking though the education was, there was obvious pride in what the teachers and students had accomplished. And a feeling that people who have come along later, including President Obama, have stood on their shoulders.

Visit us at
www.historypress.net